CW01645520

Goodbye, Dragon Inn

20
03

GOODBYE, DRAGON INN

Nick Pinkerton

Published in Australia in 2021
by Fireflies Press
www.firefliespress.com

Typography: James Geoffrey Nunn
Typeface: Alcalá by Damien Gautier, 205TF
Printed and bound by KOPA. First printing.

Distributed by
Books at Manic (Australia) and Central Books (Europe)

ISBN: 978-3-9819186-7-0

A catalogue record for this book is available from the National Library of Australia

The Decadent Editions series is generously supported by our Publishing Partner, ACMI: the museum of screen culture.

For my mother, Maura Lohman

Author's note

In late December of 2019, I put the finishing touches on the first draft of this book, on the subject of Tsai Ming-liang's 2003 film *Goodbye, Dragon Inn*, which I regard as a key text of 21st-century moving image-based art. In choosing my subject, I was guided by the belief that Tsai's film was sufficiently rich to sustain a book-length analysis, for though it has only the most bare-bones of narratives, it is nevertheless chock-a-block with ideas, touching on preoccupations central to his practice in the years before and after its making, as well as issues crucial to the future of cinema, whatever may now be said to constitute "cinema".

Tsai is a filmmaker of cities, and fast-changing Taipei, the setting of *Goodbye, Dragon Inn*, is the one to which he has returned most frequently, to find it different every time. At the centre of that film is the story of the life and death of a particular kind of urban institution, the neighbourhood cinema, a social space whose existence brings with it the possibility of both communal artistic experience and the chance encounter. (These encounters tend not to end happily in his films, but such intersections, and the promises and disappointments of urban life, are nevertheless a source of touching fascination to him.) The film has the feeling of a lingering glance following a beloved object as it slowly recedes in the distance, and if it seems somehow prescient today, it's because Tsai was well ahead of the curve in recognising that monumental shifts were in store for moviegoing practice.

A scant couple of months after I'd submitted that first draft, the spread of Covid-19 inspired governments the world over to respond with the mass shuttering of not only cinemas but shops, art galleries, bars, restaurants, gyms, concert halls, sport stadiums and practically any public space which acts as a staging ground for human meetings and congregations, and therefore was reckoned as a potential vector for infection. Amidst the panic and plague times pessimism, artworks that could "speak to the moment" were sought after, and Tsai was not unrepresented in social media conversation. With the movie theatre now facing a real existential threat, *Goodbye, Dragon Inn* seemed all the more bittersweet – the Cinema Worker Solidarity Fund, which raised money for New York City's out-of-a-job theatre employees, used an image from the film on their GoFundMe page. Likewise being mentioned anew was 1998's *The Hole*, a film set in a Taipei that has been largely abandoned following the outbreak of a mysterious disease, concerning two occupants of an emptied-out apartment building who communicate through a gradually widening breach between her floor and his ceiling. Long before the term became ubiquitous, Tsai had made social distancing his great subject.

At the time of this writing, the movie theatres remain dark in New York City, where I live, and the timetable for a reopening – or the economic viability of their reopening, with only a fraction of seats available for use – is uncertain. Many closures of businesses large and small have already been announced, and many, many more are to be expected. Such a catastrophe may seem to demand a reconsideration of what had been written in the days before its coming, but in re-reading my text I find that no such revision, beyond this introduction, appears necessary. A catastrophe, natural or man-made – this pandemic is a bit of both – doesn't generate crises out of thin air, but rather expedites our arrival at a traumatic break that brings all manner of heretofore underlying issues to the point of emergency. Now, in 2020, as crowd control edicts have rendered "the multitudes" a concept fraught with anxiety, almost none of the once-so-permanent-seeming institutions whose existence was contingent on the regular gathering of crowds, in the form of audiences, look to be safe from total disappearance.

For some companies, as well as individuals, this turn of events may not be received as an unendurable loss – it may even be, quietly, welcome. The streaming video giants, including Netflix, whose co-CEO Reed Hastings has in unguarded moments been quite forthright about regarding theatrical exhibitors as competition to be eliminated, have been handed months of captive audiences as cinemas stand empty. While quarantine and shutdown were experienced by some as an unpleasant or worse disruption from normal life, for others they will only have helped excuse commitment to a lifestyle of all-encompassing domestic consumerism that has already reached advanced stages of development, as men and women shop and consume their "content" – including cinema – via app. Without the messiness and unpredictability that comes of participating in the street life of a city, you eat via Seamless, date via Tinder and fulfil most any other need via Amazon. Not only is it increasingly convenient not to have to leave the house and 'wed the crowd', in Charles Baudelaire's famous formulation, now to remain chaste from the rabble can be construed as a righteous act.

The present crisis poses an imminent danger to the established order; it also poses an opportunity. Already-looming threats to certain notions of the function of shared public space are very much central to *Goodbye, Dragon Inn*. In his subsequent work, Tsai has become increasingly interested in exploring the opportunities for cinema, the medium, which have arisen from the imperilment of cinemas. (When I speak of cinemas I am not at this juncture referring to those multiplex monstrosities that dedicate their sixteen screens almost entirely to tentpole blockbusters directed by corporate committee; these only rarely today happen to screen anything that could be described as cinema.)

For all of these reasons, *Goodbye, Dragon Inn* is singularly suited to a culture – film culture specifically, but not only – in flux. And Tsai is an artist in a class by himself in his continuing dedication to understanding the ongoing changes to the medium, repurposing his practice to suit the possibilities of a conception of cinema that has forever been changing but in the twenty-first century has threatened to change beyond recognition. Like his film, what I have written here can stand as an epitaph for moviegoing as we have known it. Like him – if I may be so presumptive as to extrapolate from what he has said – I believe that no art form born to the world has ever disappeared from it, and that any “death of cinema” perforce must be followed by rebirth. Speaking only for myself, I don’t know if I believe that what follows this calamity can be better than what came before, but I intend to act as if I do.

Goodbye, Dragon Inn

1.

I remember as if it were yesterday, if I remember right. It was 1997, I was sixteen years old, and I was leaving the Tri-County 1–5 in Springdale, Ohio, one of the northern suburbs of Cincinnati, with my friend Adam, with whom I had just seen Mark A.Z. Dippé's *Spawn*.

The movie itself, mind you, is a bit of a blur; I've retained the rudimentary details at most. I'm not champing at the bit for a rewatch, but with reasonable confidence I can tell you a few things about it. For example, the soundtrack was made up of pairings of electronic musicians and rock bands, something like the odd-couple novelty premise behind the hip-hop/rock act collisions that'd made the *Judgment Night* soundtrack a Billboard chart presence four years earlier. At that moment in time we were between the *Mortal Kombat* (1995) theme getting heavy radio play and the 1999 phenomenon that was Moby's *Play*; there was a sense "techno" was going to finally break big in the US mainstream – which it finally did, though as back-up music for pop vocalists. I can say with some certitude, also, that the movie was based on comic books created by the Canadian artist and writer Todd McFarlane, and that it features John Leguizamo as the film's heavy, a morbidly obese clown who's possibly a demon of some kind? Like I said, it's a little foggy, the memory having begun to evaporate the minute I was back in the open air again, as do the memories of so many movies, leaving in time just a faint oily residue in the brainpan.

What I do remember, though, is the feeling I had while watching *Spawn*, and the conversation Adam and I had after the fact in the theatre's parking lot, lingering by his 1983 hatchback Honda Civic. I was trying to shake off the listlessness and disorientation of the last ninety-six minutes, as well as a sense of detachment that I couldn't remember experiencing at the movies before – or at least not to such an acute degree that I was compelled to articulate it, as I did then – something akin to what you'd get from watching someone else play a video game without participating. Every generation may perchance experience at some point this sense of alienation in the face of the medium's technological changes: for film theorist Rudolf Arnheim and contemporaries, the cinema's potential as an art form largely ended with the coming of the Talkies; for the Boomer counterculture critics, Steven Spielberg was Satan incarnate, the revenge of Rockwellian repression, a hawker of tie-in toys and pre-packaged arcade game levels. What one generation perceives as catastrophe, the next takes as the natural state of things and the medium marches on.

This, however, was the first time I could positively identify the faint, fluttering feeling of obsolescence that would become a familiar companion in years to come, a premonition of popular culture walking across my grave. It was still a period of uneasy acclimation for those of us not raised as digital natives, computer-generated imagery not yet having become ubiquitous. Four years had passed since Spielberg's *Jurassic Park*, whose touted CGI was integrated with a heaping helping of practical effects work, and still the new effects just as often came out looking awful as awestriking. The week before *Spawn*, I'd likely seen a particularly bracing instance of the awful – because in those days, without discrimination, I saw practically every new release the week it went into theatres – in the plane crash that climaxes Wolfgang Petersen's otherwise enjoyably insipid *Air Force One*, a splashdown that looks like a cutscene from a Sega CD game. (At the same time that movies were starting to resemble video games, some were convinced the future of gaming would be more cinematic; see for instance "interactive movie" game *Night Trap*.)

So Adam and I talked about this feeling of alienation and he said something to the effect of 'Movies aren't going to work the same way in a few years. They're going to be something different.' This is not an earth-shaking insight; a teenager at any time in the twentieth century could have said something to this effect and they would have been correct, or correct enough. Film history is borne along by technological innovation, and by ructions in business models, and by the whims of the viewing public as ineffably impacted by broader socio-historical-political trends, and by countless other vagaries that ensure no two generations of cinema are ever exactly the same. And then, too, as time passes, one must endeavour to discriminate between changes that have taken place in cinema and changes that have taken place in one's self. I could not imagine, for example, enduring every new multiplex release in the 2010s as I did in 1997 – not just *Spawn* and *Air Force One* but Luis Llosa's *Anaconda*, Dennis Dugan's *Beverly Hills Ninja*, Jeff Pollack's *Booty Call*... That I no longer exercise the same omnivorous (or, more accurately, indifferent) moviegoing practices has nothing to do with the movies getting worse – maybe they have, but that's neither here nor there – and everything to do with the changing demands on my time and patience, and perhaps a creeping comprehension of my own mortality.

Nevertheless, it strikes me in retrospect that this 'They're going to be something different' truism – the times, they are a-changin'! – was at that particular moment truer than usual. A thread that connected a century of cinema history was about to be snipped. The thread was the celluloid film strip, the employment of which stretched back in an unbroken line to the genesis of the medium in the 1890s, when Louis Lumière apocryphally pronounced his newborn invention stillborn, dubbing it 'an invention without a future'. The film strip was the very material of the motion picture medium, its oil and canvas, so central that we still speak of 'films' and 'filming' even as moviemaking is largely now a process conducted in part or in whole in the digital ether. On the level of post-production, the filmmaking process – there I go, doing it – was already well on its way to near-total digitisation come the close of the 1990s. In the years ahead, this changeover would gradually encompass first the processes of production, as more and more filmmakers experimented with increasingly mobile and high resolution digital cameras, then of distribution and exhibition, as the analogue film print and projector gave way to the digital projector and Digital Cinema Package (DCP), a packing crate for video and audio files contained on a portable hard drive, no larger than a *Jurassic Park* lunchbox. The avatar for this change – long anticipated, but expedited at his insistence – was a 2009 blockbuster by a rangy megalomaniac from Ontario, who in the year of *Spawn* had re-sunk the *RMS Titanic* to enormous profit.

This was, on the level of distribution and exhibition at least, a huge improvement in convenience over the nightmarish logistics of print trafficking, which involved pricey physical prints being juggled in constant circulation, using dingy warehouse depots in places like Rahway, New Jersey and hefty, rust-mottled Goldberg Bros. film canisters, with little room for error and any mishap a costly one. DCP was easier. DCP was cheaper. DCP could be projected for a whole multiplex by a teenager zoning out to PornHub (and usually is). And when dollars and cents clash with intangibles like ambiance or texture or "aura", when have the intangibles ever carried the day?

Today, on every front, in an almost comprehensive rout, the analogue has lost ground to the digital. The bound book and print magazine have faced competition from tablet and laptop, the CD collection has been replaced by the Spotify subscription. (Vinyl, meanwhile, holds the line with a niche audiophile market.) Descendants of rock groups of the sort represented on the *Spawn* soundtrack – Marilyn Manson, Korn, Metallica – still rehearse in basements and play in bars across the Republic, but have largely ceased to streak across the firmament of international pop culture or fill arenas, and small band music built around an amplified live human performance occupies today an increasingly marginal and localised cultural space, like that once reserved for the traditional folk music forms from which it derives. The clash between pop and a villainised rock'n'roll is dramatised in 2020's *Trolls World Tour*, a film with the palette of puked-up Tropical Skittles, courtesy DreamWorks Animation, one of a host of entities that specialise in turning out the CGI cartoons that have largely displaced hand-drawn cel and stop-motion animation. (Released simultaneously in theatres and video-on-demand in the early months of the pandemic, the DreamWorks picture was seen largely through digital rentals, an event that some observers perceived as another augury of the end of theatrical moviegoing.)

The enormity of this shift has not gone unobserved. In his *Film After Film: Or, What Became of 21st Century Cinema?*, J. Hoberman reckons that a defining feature of the new millennium's moving image-based art has been the degree to which the development of CGI 'broke the special relationship that existed between photography and the world'. In other words, somewhere between the appearance of Photoshop in 1990 and the present deepfake era, through the refinement of technology that can imitate life with photorealistic precision, the indexical relationship between the camera and the reality it captures has become hopelessly complicated. André Bazin, in his 1946 essay 'The Myth of Total Cinema', put forth that the 'guiding myth' behind the invention of cinema was a reaching towards 'an integral realism, a recreation of the world in its own image, an image unburdened by the freedom of interpretation of the artist or the irreversibility of time.' What has in fact transpired in the 21st-century development of the medium, at least in its big-budget manifestations, is nearer to what was exhorted by the critic Kenneth Tynan in a journal entry:

> I am certain that the full potential of the cinema will not be achieved until it concentrates on the development of *full-length cartoons* ... I do not, by this, mean stylised drawings of talking animals; nor would anyone imagine anything so absurd were it not for the fact that Walt Disney's accidental domination of the cartoon scene has made it impossible for us to think of it except in terms of clothed, speaking animals ...
>
> What the cinema ought to be doing (and to have done) is to present coloured *images* of reality (or fantasy) designed by *artists*. At present – by using the camera merely to photograph *reality* – it is confining itself to a function that is part newsreel and part photographed theatre. In pure cinema there would be no real actors and no real backgrounds; there would be drawn (or painted) people in drawn (or painted) settings. Only thus will cinema achieve its historic mission of rising above and eventually replacing the novel.

Disney's domination is no less felt now than it was when Tynan was writing in 1972, but much of what he wrote has come to pass, as blockbusters arrive at market with their every image digitally sweetened, colour palettes graded to orange and teal for maximum pop on the LCD screen. That feeling evoked by *Spawn*, of watching someone else playing video games, is now not only pervasive in the cinema but sought out elsewhere in the form of Twitch streams, a massively popular field of home entertainment, reported in 2018 to have eclipsed the audience for traditional, that is, physical, spectator sports. The old is, if not definitively dying, contested at every turn by the new. In a scant few years, the very viability of the venerable theatrical rollout model has been challenged by the rise of streaming giants bankrolling "cinematic" spectacles that can be conveniently viewed on your laptop, tablet or smartphone.

In spite of the streaming onslaught, the multiplexes have to date abided – and, thanks to DCP's low overhead and convenient transportability, in greater numbers worldwide than ever before. Never has it been so easy for transnational corporations to throw up a new eighteen-screener in some far-flung corner of the globe and to keep their hundreds or even thousands of screens (Beijing-based Wanda Group alone owns around fifteen thousand) supplied with what is now known colloquially as "content" – the noun suggests the adjective, and the attendant implication of sated passivity. The nature of that content has changed accordingly, as the major studios concentrate on $100M+ franchise tentpoles sheared of cultural specificities for maximum seamless exportability, leading to a sense that in America, at least, the mid-budget middle range of cinema – the surest marker of a healthy pop cinema ecosystem – is at risk of disappearing almost entirely.

An art form that has traditionally required the use of prohibitively costly tools, cinema in the capitalist world has from its inception been shaped by the demands of commerce – those working under a regime rather than a corporation, meanwhile, must negotiate their own compromises. Such a thing as a free filmmaker has never existed, be it in Beijing or Hollywood or Timbuktu, and no small part of film scholarship consists of elucidating how artists have managed to function *as artists* within these imposed strictures, the proof that they've done so being readily found in the works they've left behind.

Thus ever has it been and, presumably, ever will it be. Among film history-literate observers there's an eternal impulse to respond to any "unprecedented" change by pleading Ecclesiastes 1:9, reminding us with a serene smile that there is nothing new under the sun. But to do so is to blinker ourselves to the fact that these are, in some respects, unprecedented times. Profit margins are unprecedented – at least for the Walt Disney Company under recently exited CEO Bob Iger. By investing in proven intellectual property rather than nurturing relationships with above-the-line talent, Disney has taken a volatile industry and given it for the first time in history a predictable rate of return, making themselves the envy of and model for the modern Hollywood movie studio.

I am not alone in having an uneasy sense that this environment – in which profligate extravagancy is the rule rather than the exception, and the relentless mining of data and fan service feedback reinforces an existing inclination to risk aversion among those who've put money on the line – offers less and less wiggle room for anything eccentric or personal or intuitive to make its way into pop filmmaking. Increasingly, going to the multiplex has felt like witnessing the execution of bullet-pointed instructions on a front office memorandum rather than a creative collaboration by human beings.

To those who bemoan the state-of-the-art-by-committee as it exists today on the industrial scale, there is perhaps some hope in the democratisation of the filmmaking process. Making a movie, if all you want to do is make it, is less than ever a killingly costly proposition. Film and lab fees are no longer an intrinsic, budget-devouring part of the ordeal, and the rudimentary tools are now available to anyone with a smartphone. But a few success stories, critical (Sean Baker's 2015 *Tangerine*) or financial (Oren Peli's 2007 *Paranormal Activity*), do not an industry shake-up make. Just because you can go out and make your movie for peanuts doesn't mean it will be seen in a cinema – or not, at least, outside of the film festival rounds, which have become a de facto distribution circuit, though one without mechanics in place to allow artists to turn a profit.

Is this ceding of the popular conception of cinema to corporate entities necessarily a tragedy? The critic Kent Jones seems not to think so in a 2016 piece for *Film Comment* titled 'The Marginalization of Cinema', which recognises the surrender of the medium's privileged place in the public imagination. Jones writes:

> The conversation about cinema was, for many years, as big and broad as its place in the culture, but it's possible that we are now at the point where even the word 'conversation' has lost its meaning. Cinema is destined to be shared, and made, in a whole new way. The conditions of the art form as we've known it and come to love it are dying, but there will be no death of cinema. Rather, it is in the process of being culturally marginalized, which means that it is assuming a proud place alongside poetry, dance, and concert music.

Jones appears resigned to and even rather content with this development, concluding, with a well-placed qualification: 'You might even say that the marginalization of the cinema will be its salvation.' I confess that I find the prospect more depressing than liberating, as one who as a young man gravitated towards cinema rather than poetry, dance or concert music because it seemed both remote from official school culture and accessible to regular punters in a way those things did not, or at least that's how I've come to explain it to myself after the fact.

While almost no one would deny that ours is a time of enormous disruption and turbulence in film culture, diagnoses as to what precisely is happening vary. Future scholars trying to understand moving image-based art in our day could do worse than studying a 2013 curio produced by the critic-cum-filmmaker and known shit-stirrer Paul Schrader for the 70th Venice International Film Festival. Wearing a rig that suspends four GoPro cameras from his body and grants him a more than slight resemblance to Spider-Man villain

Doctor Octopus, a sweaty Schrader shoulders his way through oncoming tourists on Manhattan's High Line park – that crown jewel of Bloomberg New York, a formerly functioning piece of infrastructure prettified into public space – while reeling off a monologue about cinema in 'a time of crisis'. Beginning with the social upheaval of the late sixties and early seventies that produced the 'new heroes' of New Hollywood – himself, incidentally, among them – Schrader moves on to what he identifies as the 'crisis of form' in the present moment. 'We don't know quite what movies are,' he says.

> We don't know how long they are, we don't know how you see them, where you see them, how you pay for them. It feels more like 1913 than 2013. Everything is being made up on the fly. The idea of film entertainment is undergoing a systematic change. Every week brings another change. No one knows for sure what it'll be like. It won't be a projected image in a dark room in front of the audience. That's twentieth century.

Schrader was at Venice with his film of that same year, *The Canyons*, his old dog's new trick, and the circumstances of its much-publicised production and distribution – financed via Kickstarter and released direct to video-on-demand services – reflect those systemic changes. The movie opens with what is intended as a moratorium for the brick-and-mortar cinema: a montage of still images of multiplexes fallen into rack and ruin, their parking lots fissured and pocked, clues as to the identity of their final screenings given by a few changeable letters still clinging to their signage. The Tri-County where I saw *Spawn* might very well have been included in that roll call of the departed. Passed between chains through its life, from Mid-States Theaters to Loew's to National Amusements, it was closed down sometime after I'd left Cincinnati in the early 2000s, and demolished shortly thereafter.

Schrader's eulogy *feels* correct, but in other regards it's premature, if not outright deceptive. Old multiplexes have faced the wrecking ball, yes, but new ones have sprung up to take their place, just as the 'plexes once replaced the single-screen houses. These state-of-the-art temples of commerce are shiny, well-appointed buildings fitted with reclining leather seats and RPX-equipped theatres and liquor-licensed concession stands, extending to the consumer all the comforts of home and more in a bid to lure them away from their flat screens. And spending an exorbitantly expensive evening in one of these buildings hasn't yet ceased to be a sought after activity – or, at any rate, robber barons like Iger and their various lieutenants continue to rake in the chips.

How can cinema be dead when business is booming? This depends on how we define cinema. Jones builds a contrast between 'audiovisual spectacle', that 'succession of ruthlessly calibrated, wind tunnel-tested, wholly interchangeable slabs of worldwide entertainment that roll off the assembly line year by year' of the sort specialised in by the franchise-oriented studios, and *cinema*. The latter he defines as an art of compression where 'every choice becomes charged and interacts with every other choice in the momentum toward a defined end point' – this in contrast to "quality" serial television, touted as the new refuge of Serious Adult Drama – as well as an art whose essence is to be found not in maximalist blockbuster bluster but in 'nuances and the tiniest shifts in rhythm and suspended harmonies that seem to have been struck on a tuning fork and allowed to gradually degrade.'

Some years after *The Canyons*, Schrader and Jones's old confrere Martin Scorsese generated a good bit of copy for the ever-desperate-for-a-story cultural commentariat when, in doing the press rounds leading up to the release of his Netflix-financed *The Irishman* (2019) – a film which flaunts Bazin's assertions on the 'irreversibility of time' – he commented that the Marvel Studios movies made under the aegis of Disney were more akin to amusement park rides than cinema, and then doubled down on the assertion in a *New York Times* op-ed. (As fate would have it, Iger's successor as Disney CEO, Bob Chapek, would be the former chair of the company's parks and resorts division, who presided over the opening of the Shanghai Disney Resort.)

For some, this hand-wringing has less to do with the health of cinema than it does with the demographic expressing it: Jones, Scorsese, Schrader and, yes, your faithful author are all

Americans, all hetero cis males, and all varying degrees of old and varying shades of Caucasian. Might not these pronouncements of marginalisation and crisis be linked to a sense of growing personal obsolescence, an awareness of a loss of market share?

It's a caveat worth expressing, but it doesn't change the basic fact of the medium's turmoil. Concurrent but unrelated to incremental demographic shifts in who is making films – an unalloyed good – and the composition of the increasingly borderless audience that the big-budget ones, at least, are being addressed to, this has been a period of tectonic shifts in our understanding of, as Schrader says, what movies are. For approximately the first half of its lifespan, 'cinema' bore a double meaning: it was both the medium, and the place where you went to see it. Television and home video troubled this affiliation between place and art form – in point of fact, the exceptional film literacy of Schrader and Scorsese's Movie Brat generation is as much as anything else attributable to the prevalence of old movies on television. The internet eroded that affiliation to the point where fundamental questions of identity are now being relitigated. Is *Twin Peaks: The Return* cinema? Is Beyoncé's *Lemonade*? Are the films of Wang Bing, many of them durational epics, frequently shown abroad in a gallery context and seen in his native China mostly on circulated samizdat-style files, if at all? Once an aristocrat among moving image-based arts by dint of sheer size and cultural import, cinema has by gradual measures been brought down to earth through a great levelling, as often as not today viewed by audiences on the same screens that serve them up series "television" old and new, makeup tutorials, music clips, Li Ziqi cooking YouTube videos, *Red Dead Redemption 2*, and so forth.

Supreme Court Justice Potter Stewart's famous definition of pornography – 'I know it when I see it' – is insufficient to establish parameters for an art form. Amidst new uncertainty, we must pose again the question asked by Bazin's collected works: What is cinema? It is here that *Goodbye, Dragon Inn* (2003), and the cinema of Tsai Ming-liang, can be of enormous service.

2.

Some years before most of us were fully awake to the need for such a redefinition of terms, the Taiwanese writer-director Tsai was already on the case. His *Goodbye, Dragon Inn*, a work of profound sensitivity and intuition, seemed to understand something essential about the changing of the cinematic playing field, at a time when few grasped how radically the lines were going to be redrawn.

Save for a brief prologue, *Goodbye, Dragon Inn* takes place in a contemporary turn-of-the-millennium Taipei, and entirely on the premises or in the immediate vicinity of a movie theatre that has seen better days, the Fu-Ho Grand, on the course of a single rainy night, during the course of a single screening, the evening's last: King Hu's

1967 *Dragon Inn*, aka *Dragon Gate Inn*. A canonical instance of the *wuxia* cinema, which depicts martial artist heroes in an ancient and usually rustic China of lore, Hu's film maintains a somewhat phantom-like presence throughout Tsai's: *Dragon Inn* is glimpsed upon the Fu-Ho screen, and its distinctive soundtrack is near-constantly audible both inside the cinema hall and out.

Goodbye, Dragon Inn, however, is focused in the main on the activities of the patrons and employees of the cinema, in particular two: a ticket seller, played by Tsai regular Chen Shiang-chyi, hobbled by a clunky, noisy leg brace that makes her routine trip up the stairs a painstaking and agonising-looking affair; and a male Japanese tourist, played by Mitamura Kiyonobu, who drifts throughout the theatre, scrutinising the other audience members for, we soon ascertain, possible same-sex companionship. The film in essence is a string of vignettes, detailing the largely private, largely taciturn activities of the cinema's denizens. Chen takes her lunch in the ticket booth, setting aside half of a steamed pink bun to deliver later as a gift to the projectionist, an unseen presence through much of the film who appears finally in the last reel, played by Tsai's muse, Lee Kang-sheng. Kiyonobu roves the premises, avoiding noisy eaters and other violators of moviegoing etiquette while pursuing an agenda that has little to do with the film on screen.

More attentive to the feature are two older patrons, played by stars of Hu's *Dragon Inn*: Shih Chun, formerly the wandering swordsman Xiao Shao-zi; and Miao Tien, the actor who portrayed his nemesis, Pi Shao-tang, commander of the Eastern Depot secret police – the latter in his fifth film for Tsai. These older men watch the film unspool intently, or as intently as is possible through eyes fogged by nostalgia. Miao has with him a very young grandson, who alone in the crowd seems to be wholly *there* to the movie, the only spectator really seeing the film (his first?) without his attention diluted by distractions of one kind or another. As the movie closes, the two men meet in the lobby and greet one another by their own given names, their exchange making it explicit they are in fact playing themselves, two forgotten screen stars who have come to gaze upon their younger selves writ large for perhaps the last time.

Their conversation, which lasts for all of six lines, is the most extensive to take place in the world of the Fu-Ho. Such moments of person-to-person contact are, throughout, brief – for the curious double nature of moviegoing, both a communal and a deeply private, solitary activity, is very much at the heart of *Goodbye, Dragon Inn*. Palaver between theatre patrons being at a bare minimum, the great majority of the speech heard in the film is ambiance, coming from the soundtrack of *Dragon Inn*, and it isn't until just after the halfway point that a character, played by Chen Chao-jung, another repeat Tsai player, speaks a line of original dialogue.

In style, too, Tsai's film could be described as reserved in the extreme. Camera movements are few and understated, and cuts are rare and purposeful, with scenes often observing a character from before their entrance into the frame and after their exit from it. All of this is consistent with a greater and greater limitation of stylistic tools that had been underway throughout Tsai's five features up to this point. As such it is near to the diametric opposite of Hu's film, which fairly vibrates with swashbuckling cinematographic verve, relishing in the synchronous interplay between music and the motion of both actors and camera. In the dark, cool, quiet setting provided by Tsai, one catches the occasional glimmer from Hu's glittering, glinting particolored gem of a film, shining in the lowered lights.

Goodbye, Dragon Inn premiered at the Venice Film Festival, bested in competition for the Golden Lion by Andrey Zvyagintsev's *The Return*. Since the appearance of 1992's *Rebels of the Neon God* – Tsai's first theatrical feature, though he had been working in television movies previously – he had slowly but surely, feature by feature, established himself as a major international director with a distinct and recognisable style and worldview and, at least in niche arthouse terms, a modestly bankable brand. *Goodbye, Dragon Inn* was distributed in the US by Wellspring Media, which during the film's theatrical run in fall of 2004 had been newly acquired by the Las Vegas-based American

Vantage Media, whose then-vice chairman was none other than short-lived White House chief strategist Steve Bannon. It's unknown as to if Bannon ever sat down in a screening room to look over his company's latest acquisition, though the imagination certainly reels at the possibility.

Wellspring did a not-half-bad job of getting *Goodbye, Dragon Inn* out there. My grandfather in New Smyrna Beach, Florida saw it of his own volition, and on getting this news I thought for sure that Tsai was on the verge of becoming, if not a household name, then at least a confirmed arthouse star. Not on the level of a Fellini or a Bergman or a Truffaut, mind you – there simply weren't arthouse celebrities on that level anymore, which one supposes must be indicative of something – but maybe somewhere between, say, Wong Kar-wai, the dorm room darling of the fin-de-millennium whose *In the Mood for Love* had been a bona fide cult hit, and Edward Yang, whose *Yi Yi* (both 2000), distributed by Wellspring predecessor Winstar, had gotten a theatrical run in the medium-sized market town of Cincinnati, something which today seems like science fiction.

At this moment, it was these Pacific Rim filmmakers from territories in what has sometimes been referred to as Greater China – here, Tsai and Yang's Taiwan and Wong's Hong Kong – who seemed poised most precisely and precariously on the edge of contemporaneity, who seemed best situated to explain where precisely we in the industrialised and post-industrialised world were and were going as we approached the Y2K deadline. As residents of these cosmopolite refugee territories, they were accustomed to the bewilderment of cultural dislocation, the social isolation resultant from the dissolution of traditional community ties, and the transitory nature of life lived in teeming transit lounge cities, subject to constant construction and destruction under the conditions of hypercapitalist overdrive.

Looking warily to the future, Tsai's film begins in the past. The prologue of *Goodbye, Dragon Inn* mentioned above takes place within the confines of the same cinema, the Fu-Ho Grand, and also during a screening of Hu's *Dragon Inn*. There is, however, an immediately perceptible difference between the Fu-Ho seen here and that in the rest of the film: it's alive. Tsai's opening credits are accompanied by, first, the blast of fanfare that introduces Hu's film, then the narration, which identifies the scene of its action. It's 1457 AD, smack in the middle of the Ming Dynasty, and the peasantry live in terror of marauding bands led by scheming eunuchs and their agents – a time of chaos in the kingdom, introducing a movie that addresses film culture amidst revolutionary confusion.

A glimpse of *Dragon Inn* fills the screen: a palanquin carries the chief of the eunuchs, Cao Shao-qin (Bai Ying), who dismounts to stroll to a dais on a raised platform. Then, quite suddenly, we are outside of the movie – or, rather, the movie that we've been introduced to is revealed to be part of another. A thick curtain parts, giving onto a view of the cinema in which every seat is occupied, the full house in thrall to the film's imperious images and skirling music – a soundtrack inspired by Peking opera, featuring the *sheng* reed pipe, *di* bamboo flute and crashing percussion.

After offering a few angles of the room to capture the magnitude of the sold-out crowd, the frame settles into a curious composition, behind the heads of two figures near the front of the cinema. One appears to be male, with a shaved head and spectacles – two features associated with Tsai, though the figure registers as adolescent – seated next to his rather larger neighbour, gender undetermined, who has a shock of unruly grey hair. The face of neither is seen, and they will play no further role in the movie as characters. They read as grandchild and grandmother, a mirror of the little grandchild and Miao in the film's present-day section. They also suggest another grandparent-grandchild couple, without which *Goodbye, Dragon Inn* wouldn't exist, for the boy, after a fashion, is Tsai Ming-liang.

3.

Years later, successfully established as a filmmaker, Tsai would recount his initial encounter with Hu's film:

> I first saw *Dragon Inn* when I was eleven years old. A record-breaking hit, it impressed me the most among the hundreds of martial arts films I saw as a child. The sound of the vertical flute in the film made me feel for the first time the vastness and loneliness of the world of knights-errant. In other martial arts films, the characters fly around and tread freely on roofs and walls. Only King Hu's knights-errant walk the lonely path in desolate mountains. Some say King Hu chose a lonely and difficult road of filmmaking, but this is precisely what makes his films unforgettable.

That impactful screening would not have taken place in the Fu-Ho Grand in Taipei or indeed anywhere in Taiwan, where Tsai would be based through his adult life, but in his hometown of Kuching, Sarawak, Malaysia, a city on the island of Borneo with a population of around 750,000 in 1960, a little under one-third of that ethnic Chinese, like Tsai's family.

Tsai was born in 1957 – eight years after the decisive victory of the People's Liberation Army (PLA) in the Chinese Civil War that sent refugees streaming into Taiwan, Hong Kong and points beyond, and the year of the Malaysian proclamation of independence from Britain at Stadium Merdeka in Kuala Lumpur – and he spent the first twenty years of his life in Kuching, living through the founding of the Independent Federation of Malaysia in 1963. His parents were farmers who also operated a noodle stall, and after the birth of his younger brother he was principally looked after by his grandparents, described by Tsai in 2016 as 'the biggest cinephiles I knew'. Hence, it's not too much to infer, the grey head at the beginning of *Goodbye, Dragon Inn*. Of his early cinematic education with those grandparents, Tsai wrote, 'We started going to movies together when I was three years old. We would go to the cinema twice a day, every day. Sometimes we would watch the same film over and over again, and sometimes we would find different cinemas to watch something new. That was a golden age for cinema, and I'm proud my childhood coincided with that time.'

He grew up during the years when a Sinophone film industry most notably centred in Hong Kong was servicing a widespread Chinese diaspora community, years that produced a robust popular culture which to this day attracts legions of devotees, both in Greater China and elsewhere. Access to the Mainland Chinese market was unpredictable after the victory of Mao Zedong's PLA in 1949 (except for those studios with explicitly left-wing, pro-Beijing sympathies, like Hong Kong's Great Wall Movie Enterprises Limited) which meant that the burgeoning markets of Hong Kong and Taiwan and other Chinese émigré hubs and destinations would become ever more closely entwined. For half a century, Hong Kong was reliant upon these various diaspora destinations to render their frantic filmmaking output profitable.

Kuching was certainly part of the circuit, and Tsai would remember the city of his youth as a place of 'about a dozen cinemas in which [he] lingered.' Very likely these would have included the Art Deco Rex in Wayang Street (presently serving as a multi-storey parking garage and the Star Cineplex) and the Sylvia Cinema, the city's first, built in 1934 and named for the wife of the third and last White Rajah of the Raj of Sarawak. Tsai singled out two cinemas in particular as having been the centre of his young filmgoing life: 'One was Capitol, which was always showing films by the Shaw Brothers Studio. The other was the Odeon, playing dialect films in Cantonese and Taiwanese, as well as some Tarzan and Godzilla serial films. Both theaters were surrounded by barbed wire. They were demolished probably seven or eight years ago.'

The memory of the Odeon recurs in Tsai's interviews from around the release of *Goodbye, Dragon Inn*. 'The ceiling was very high up and there were many fans hanging above,' he recalled.

'There were more than a thousand seats and the drapes on the side doors would drift about.' This description precedes a discussion of the ticket clerk at the Odeon, 'a crippled man' and an inspiration for the character played by Chen.

The moviegoing culture of Kuching during the years of Tsai's youth is seen through rose-tinted lenses in an article by one Alan Lau for local magazine *Kuching In & Out*. 'Kuching's cinemas were its secular temples,' Lau writes, 'drawing the faithful of all ages, all races, all backgrounds. If cinema was a religion, it was a truly democratic one. Poor and rich, young and old, all were welcome, regardless of age, occupation or religion; anyone who could afford to part with a fistful of pocket change (and quite a few who didn't) was given access behind the thick velvet curtains' – much the same drapes, presumably, that Tsai mentions in his recollection of the Odeon, and akin to those parted to afford us our first glimpse of the packed house at the beginning of *Goodbye, Dragon Inn*. Lau goes into rhapsodies describing the Rex, and in particular the comestibles offered for sale in the theatre and nearby.

> Cross the tiled foyer to the ticket counter; a few coins bought you access in the form of a brightly coloured ticket the consistency of toilet paper; you couldn't get it wet lest it stained your clothes and sent mum into hysterics. A few more coins, earnestly begged, could buy you a host of supplementary pleasures – steaming hot kacang [a hard-shelled seed] in newspaper cones, melon seeds, peanuts, and bottled soft drinks in lurid colours that hinted at the cinematic treasures to come. Outside, there were other food stalls – the Rex being a community centre as much as a cinema – selling cucur [a variety of fritter], hawker treats, and toys in plastic and tin.

Such sensorially overwhelming, sensually scented origin myths abound among cinephiles, famous and otherwise, often in connection with the names of the theatres that were the scene of early infatuation, and often with a wistful addendum referring to the disappearance of those same theatres. Scorsese, gifted with an elephantine memory, has given extensive accounting of the cinemas in his life: the second-run downtown joints strung along 2nd Avenue like the Loew's Commodore, where he had his formative first encounter with Elia Kazan's *On the Waterfront* (1954), or the Stuyvesant and the Orpheum, where tickets ran around a quarter. For underground jesters George and Mike Kuchar, a formative education was to be had on the cheap at the Bronx's big houses, the RKO Chester or the Tremont Theatre. George recalls the scene in their memoir *Reflections from a Cinematic Cesspool*: 'On weekends we'd sometimes spend the whole day sitting through double features twice. We didn't always sit, though, because the theaters were like opulent playgrounds and we'd crawl under the seats or wander about the carpeted darkness.'

Several artists have, like Tsai, conjured up the memory of these formative meetings in their work. In his largely autobiographical *Pain and Glory* (2019), Pedro Almodóvar, raised in the rural Spanish town of Calzada de Calatrava, stages a theatrical monologue that reminiscences of summers spent watching movies projected on a whitewashed wall where local boys would routinely urinate on the side of the screen; 'In the cinema of my childhood it always smells of piss and jasmine, and of the summer breeze.' In Jean Eustache's 1974 film à clef *Mes petites amoureuses*, the stated intention of which was, he told Luc Moullet, 'to reconstruct [my] childhood: every wall section, every tree, every light pole,' the cinema of his youth is not neglected: at a screening of Albert Lewin's 1951 *Pandora and the Flying Dutchman*, we see twelve-year-old Eustache alter ego Daniel (Martin Loeb) taking cues from the screen and neighbouring kids, chancing a tentative grope with a girl in the balcony.

Tsai, though, deserves some sort of special prize for both loving diligence and perverse imagination in returning to his primal cinematic scene. It is one thing to hold and to treasure the memory of a movie seen for the first time very near the age of sexual awakening; it is another to, some thirty-five years later, recruit two stars of that film to appear in one of your own making, about the melancholy cruising rituals occurring in a theatre playing that same movie. All of this is, however, some ways off – there is a great deal of ground to cover between the boy in Kuching who saw *Dragon Inn* in 1967 or '68 and the middle-aged man in Taipei who made *Goodbye, Dragon Inn*

Tsai arrived in Taiwan in 1977, there to enrol in Taipei's College of Chinese Culture, today the Chinese Culture University, whose large main campus was located outside of the city proper on the Yang Ming Mountain in Yangmingshan National Park. As a *qiaosheng* (overseas college student), Tsai studied dramatic art and wrote for the stage, graduating in 1981.

The period of Tsai's studies was a pivotal one for Taiwan. In 1979, the Congress of the United States, a close ally, passed the Taiwan Relations Act, abrogating its long-standing treaty with the Republic of China (ROC) on Taiwan in exchange for a closer diplomatic relationship with the People's Republic of China (PRC) on the Mainland – in effect foreclosing any hope for the island to be recognised on the world stage as a legitimate representative of China. The millions of refugees who had quit the Mainland, perhaps expecting to be able to return home in due time from this inconvenient layover, had hereafter to accustom themselves to a new definition of home. These were also the waning years of the White Terror in the country – the period of dissident-suppressing martial law begun when the Kuomintang-ruled government (KMT) of the ROC, including President Chiang Kai-shek and around two million troops, beat a retreat to the island in 1949. Under the White Terror, the KMT were responsible for imprisoning and, in thousands of cases, executing any perceived Communist spies or opponents of the nationalist regime. Martial law would not be lifted until 1987, and two years later Hou Hsiao-hsien's *A City of Sadness* became the first Taiwanese film to openly address the KMT's many misdeeds.

These years of rapid change were the backdrop to Tsai's artistic coming of age. While Taiwanese relations were strained to non-existent during this period with both Japan and the PRC, and the cultural output of both countries was scarcely to be seen in Taiwan, Taipei was otherwise a relatively cosmopolitan city, and in university Tsai was exposed to the cream of mid-century European cinematic modernism: Michelangelo Antonioni,

Rainer Werner Fassbinder and, a figure of particular import to Tsai, François Truffaut. He volunteered as a ticket seller at the earliest editions of the Taipei Golden Horse Film Festival in order to see films for free at the main venue, Zhongshan Hall – the same venue where the Japanese forces formally surrendered Taiwan to the ROC in 1945, and where, decades later, Tsai now operates his own coffee shop, Tsai Ming-liang's Café Corridor, which includes an eighteen-seat theatre space to screen his many installation works.

Tsai supported himself during this period by delivering lunch boxes and other odd jobs. Imagining his early years in Taipei as a qiaosheng rube scraping to get by, one might think to Chen wandering the streets of Paris in *What Time Is It There?* (2001), the film Tsai made directly before *Goodbye, Dragon Inn*, and a piercing depiction of what it is to be a far-from-home urban nomad. The films this raw, bright, delicate kid from Kuching would go on to make display an enormous affinity with and sympathy for outsiders. If, following years of professional success and back-patting plaudits on the festival circuit, Tsai maintains an intimate understanding of rejection and isolation, it is not too much of a stretch to imagine that the experience of these years – a Malaysia-raised provincial alone in a city of millions, as well as a gay man in a society where same-sex desire was verboten – are to no small degree responsible.

Little information exists in English about Tsai's theatre career, begun in university, though we do have some titles: 1981's *Instant Bean Sauce Noodle*, 1982's *A Sealed Door in the Dark* and 1983's *A Wardrobe in the Room*. Tsai was the writer, stage director and lone actor in the last-named, a piece whose premise – a young man walls himself up in sequestered seclusion from the city outside – suggests an acquaintance with absurdist dramatist Eugène Ionesco, and indicates the direction of Tsai's cinematic work to come. Tsai wrote scripts for telefilms, ten in all, which are commonly excluded from his filmography, and he directed the last three of them. (In Taiwan, as in Hong Kong, where practically the whole of the late seventies/ early eighties New Wave generation was weaned on TV production, the industry has functioned as an apprenticeship programme and a feeder to the theatrical filmmaking business.)

His directorial debut, *All Corners of the World*, concerns a family who make a subsistence living from scalping movie tickets in the rapidly changing Taipei district of Ximending. It was around this time that Tsai met a young man bumming around an arcade called Lee Kang-sheng. In spite of Lee's lack of on-camera experience, Tsai took him on as an actor – some sources list him playing a small role in *All Corners of the World*, while Tsai states that they met while he was preparing his last telefilm, 1991's *Boys* – and a thirty-year collaboration and relationship began.

Lee, born in 1968, was the son of a poor family barely supported by the father's civil war benefits. Before first performing for Tsai, Lee, who'd just flunked his university entrance exams, was working a succession of mostly unskilled jobs, including lookout at the door of an illegal gambling parlour. He would become Tsai's *acteur fétiche*, playing the lead in *Boys*, a teenager who blackmails a younger boy, and appearing in all of Tsai's theatrical features thereafter – always as a character named Hsiao-kang, Lee's real-life nickname, when his character is named at all; always indigent or working casual gigs of the sort Lee might have kept taking had he not been discovered by cinema; and in the first five films found frequently in the same family apartment, that of Lee's own family, with parents played by Miao Tien and Lu Yi-ching. Years later, Tsai would analyse the nature of his attraction to Lee:

> His family, with its very classic Taiwanese structure – a father from the Mainland, married to a local Taiwanese mother – and their quintessentially Taiwanese house were all very attractive to me. Plus, his delinquency, his air of mystery, ennui, brooding silence, and slowness... the manner in which he smoked, all made me think of my strict father, who hardly spoke any words to me during my entire upbringing.

Tsai's description has the tenderness of a lover's, though he has been at times guarded about his private life and the nature of his relationship with Lee, and his recollections of his youth have been, until recently, absent of discussion of budding sexuality. The direction of the desire displayed by

Lee's various Hsiao-kangs is fluid – being most overtly same-sex oriented in *Vive L'Amour* (1994) and in *Days* (2020), which is likewise quite explicit in its depiction of sex work. While Tsai has often made work about or pertaining to queer experience, including the 1995 documentary *My New Friends*, which centres on two HIV-positive gay men, he has been reticent about identifying his cinema as queer, per se.

Shortly before the making of *Goodbye, Dragon Inn*, Tsai discussed writing characters like that played by Lee in *Vive L'Amour*, saying, 'I do not want the audience to come to the film because it's a gay film,' while in a 2016 interview he stated that 'very early on, a friend from Hong Kong who really liked my films suggested that I participate in the London LGBT Film Festival. I thanked him but I rejected the suggestion. At the time, society was very conservative and I did not want my film to be branded. But now I would not mind. It's a learning process, learning to accept homosexuality and myself.' In 2015's *Afternoon*, a two-hour documentary of a conversation between Tsai and Lee, "outed" in the film as straight and an object of unreciprocated desire for Tsai, the filmmaker openly discusses frequenting saunas for sex.

On 24 November 2018, a referendum was to come before Taiwanese voters including several items pertaining to homosexuality, among them a proposal to overturn a 2017 Constitutional Court ruling that mandated the legalisation of same-sex marriage within a two-year period. Shortly before this, at the close of the 2018 Golden Horse Film Festival, where he was presenting his experimental documentary *Your Face*, Tsai spoke publicly about his first love, another boy, and expressed his wish that his statement might have some impact on the referendum. (Same-sex marriage remained, ultimately, illegal.)

Desire, queer and otherwise, is present in Tsai's films from the first. In *Rebels of the Neon God*, Lee's character, a morose young man living with his parents, develops a fixation with a delinquent youth, Ah Tze (Chen Chao-jung), an obsession that combines wrathful anger, seeming suppressed sexual longing, and a possible projection of homophobic self-hate in his eventual expressions of rage – when he vandalises the motorcycle belonging to the object of his obsession, he spray-paints it with the word 'AIDS'. (A similar scene occurs in *All Corners of the World*, in which the teenaged daughter expresses a secret crush on a classmate by attacking his parked scooter.)

Such unrequited and often mute yearning, expressed not-infrequently through strange ventings of frustration and the practice of a voyeuristic impulse, runs through Tsai's pre-*Goodbye, Dragon Inn* films. *Vive L'Amour* depicts a tangle of entwined desire between Lee, Chen Chao-jung and Yang Kuei-mei. *The River* (1997) focuses on Hsiao-kang and his parents, a hopelessly alienated family unit of intimate strangers – the father is as aloof to his son as Tsai describes his own as having been, and the parents are sexually estranged from one another, seeking erotic outlets elsewhere. In his next feature, *The Hole* (1998), two neighbours, Lee and Yang, communicate through a slow-growing breach between the floor of his apartment and the ceiling of hers, their pettish relationship gradually evolving into faraway-so-close pining. In *What Time Is It There?*, the divide between the central characters is far greater still – the breadth of continents separates Hsiao-kang in Taipei from Chen Shiang-chyi's character, abroad in Paris.

Goodbye, Dragon Inn, too, is a film of the lovelorn: Chen's ticket seller – Tsai's old job at the Taipei Golden Horse Film Festival, mind you – coveting a moment of attention from Lee's projectionist; and the Japanese tourist, wandering the Fu-Ho in search of succour or maybe just a suck. But these yearnings exist within a larger yearning. Their unquenched desire echoes Tsai's own desire for the popular cinema of his youth – and not just the movies, but everything that goes along with them: the big neighbourhood cinemas, the communal culture of family moviegoing, the family itself, and the absolute surrender to the screen that is perhaps only possible for the very young, that perhaps can never be experienced again, not quite the same way.

4.

The fanfare that opens *Goodbye, Dragon Inn* is followed by a comedown crash. The prologue gives us a vision of the Fu-Ho in its heyday, but immediately afterwards we encounter a Fu-Ho that's anything but Grand. It's just another underpopulated declining urban theatre on the eve of a 'Temporary Closing', which one suspects management has optimistically identified as such in order to soften the blow of their establishment's inevitable quiet passing, leaving behind no next of kin when it goes. A torrential rain – a regular presence in Tsai's wringing-wet filmography – is lapping at the lobby, and there is a sense that the entire operation might soon be underwater. *Après le cinéma, le déluge.*

This temporal leap takes us from a full theatre to a nearly empty one, from the booming popular cinema of Greater China that Tsai knew in his mid-sixties youth to that same popular cinema at the turn of the millennium, now antique, an etiolated remnant of its former self. *Goodbye, Dragon Inn* has sometimes been taken as Tsai's sweeping, definitive statement on the state of cinematic art and its waning appeal, but the narrowness of the movie's focus – one film, one cinema, two screenings – ill suits it to such a purpose. In actuality, Taiwanese audiences were still very much turning out to see movies in the early aughts: Peter Jackson's *The Lord of the Rings: The Return of the King*, to take one example, grossed NT$400M (roughly US$11.5M) in the year of Tsai's film. Rather, Tsai is concerned with a specific *type* of cinema, both film (a particularly lyrical example of the heroic wuxia of the sixties, this one made in Taiwan) and physical space (the large, single-screen urban theatre).

The audience for *Dragon Inn* has changed since childhood, and so have the preoccupations of the now-adult observer. The nagging presence of sex separates the ageing Fu-Ho from the idealised cinema of a child's memory, a popular cinema seen at its prelapsarian pinnacle. The movie is only an afterthought for most of the contemporary theatregoers, pushed and pulled about by carnal need. The stowaway-peopled interior of the Fu-Ho, where boys float and brush past each other like buoys, is a ramble of aimless corridors and storage rooms crowded by sagging, soggy cardboard. All of the walls seem to be the same shade of soiled aquamarine, each corner stained with dark tendrils of water damage, and everything contributes to the overall impression of being in the hull of some great vessel off on an underbooked farewell cruise, where the muted, echoing soundtrack of *Dragon Inn* approximates the moans of a pressurised belowdecks. A few remain in a hall designed to house thousands, and the empty space takes on an eerily palpable presence of its own. When one of the Fu-Ho's occupants does finally open his mouth, it's to enquire, 'Did you know this theatre is haunted?'

The Fu-Ho had already played a part for Tsai in *What Time Is It There?*, which likewise explored the cinema's role as a cruising spot – very much an evocation of the theatre's real-life function.

Wrote Tsai: 'After declining popularity but before closing down [the Fu-Ho] was said to have a few people of the gay community patronize the place... I'm very moved by this. Though it has declined and lost its glitter and you have forgotten about the theater, it still continues a long journey and still welcomes the outsiders of society.'

In that film, Hsiao-kang's visit to the Fu-Ho is introduced by a shot very nearly identical to that which introduces us to Chen's character in *Goodbye, Dragon Inn*: the camera is in a hallway facing out towards the cinema's lobby, the women's bathroom on the right of the frame. (A found rather than constructed set, the Fu-Ho suggests or imposes certain compositional approaches – a location is not only a "character" in a film, but a collaborator of sorts.) Like *Goodbye, Dragon Inn*, *What Time Is It There?* focuses on two people and their separate, isolate timelines. In the case of the earlier film, however, there is a moment of crucial overlap. Lee, playing a street vendor selling timepieces at the skywalk at the Taipei Train Station, meets a woman, played by Chen, who is about to depart for Paris, and is in the market for a wristwatch that will keep the time at home and abroad. Purchase made, she leaves, and he stays on; the film tracks their respective, largely lonesome urban perambulations. She makes her way through a foreign city where she knows no one and doesn't speak the language. He becomes a foreigner at home by taking a plunge into Francophilia, developing an interest in French wine and cinema, and a mania for changing clocks across Taipei six hours back, to Paris time.

The Fu-Ho's big scene in *What Time Is It There?* comes when Hsiao-kang snatches a wall clock from the cinema's hallway and sits down to watch a film alone with his new acquisition. His privacy is interrupted by the appearance of a husky, bespectacled young man who has been trailing him since an earlier encounter at a shop, and plonks into the seat next to him. When Hsiao-kang moves over, the young man makes off with the clock, to lure Hsiao-kang, in pursuit, to the upstairs men's bathroom. The bathroom at first appears empty, but then one of the stalls pops open to reveal the young man with his pants down and the clock face positioned over his crotch, its hands suggestively twitching, as though manipulated by a throbbing hard-on.

The set of cagey strategies that make up this vignette – approach, withdrawal; pursuit, recoil; thrust, parry – are further elaborated and played out in touch-and-go variants throughout *Goodbye, Dragon Inn*. Once again, the Fu-Ho Grand's men's bathroom appears as a space crackling with sexual potential. The strategic choosing of seats by those wandering the nearly empty cinema hall, where elected proximity functions as an announcement of erotic interest, plays out in an even more overt context in the toilets. A fixed-camera shot, running about three minutes in length, opens on the Japanese tourist taking up a urinal next to a lone man despite the abundance of free space: a long row of unoccupied urinals recedes into the distance. The pair are then joined by a third, who sidles up beside the Japanese tourist, hemming him in on both sides. The room is silent save the sound of running water, but the tense air of expectation is broken, briefly, when a stall door opens behind them, revealing the presence of a heretofore unnoticed fourth party, who steps out, leaving the door ajar, and goes to wash his hands. As he does, a hand appears and pulls shut the stall door, announcing still another occupant of the room and the likely fact that at least someone in this theatre of choosy comparison shoppers has managed to successfully pop their cookies. Finally, a sixth man enters the bathroom, walks over to the urinals and reaches between the Japanese tourist and one of his neighbours... to retrieve a pack of cigarettes left on the sill in front of them. Another breach of etiquette, in a scene already bristling with them, its minutely calibrated sight gags suggesting a Jacques Tati who has turned his attention to a comedy of cruising manners.

Tsai's film was not alone around this time in exploring the function of the cinema as a cruising spot – Wong Kar-wai includes a boozy, woozy blowjob in a Buenos Aires cinema in his *Happy Together* (1997) and the second film by Jacques Nolot, the self-explanatorily titled *Porn Theatre*, premiered in Cannes a year before the release of *Goodbye, Dragon Inn* – carrying on a legacy of films dealing with the peculiar protocol at play in adult cinemas that runs through Marie-Claude Treilhou's *Simone Barbes or Virtue* (1980) and Bette Gordon's *Variety* (1983). Both Wong and Nolot stage their scenes in theatres heard to be playing porno movies, the onscreen action being kept out of view. Such venues are increasingly scarce in a post-home video, post-internet era, where one can easily get one's rocks off in the privacy of one's own office; these spaces continue to operate today, on the odd occasions that they do, by functioning as an arena largely dedicated to same-sex male cruising and, even in this, catering to an ageing, shrinking clientele. New York City is presently home to only two such cinemas, the Kings Highway Cinema in Gravesend and the Fair in East Elmhurst, Queens, with a third, Manhattan's underground Bijou at 82 East 4th Street, having recently closed its doors.

The Fu-Ho isn't explicitly catering to the raincoat crowd; insofar as we can tell, it is a "straight" commercial theatre, seen on the evening of a revival run – an unusual event judging from the visible posters, which include several for the Pang brothers' 2002 *The Eye* (a Hong Kong-Singapore co-production and, fittingly, another ghost story). By the early aughts there was reportedly only one cinema left in Taipei still showing "blue movies", presumably the Baixue grindhouse in Ximending, which was said to mix in Category III films from Hong Kong with straight fare, and was a popular cruising destination prior to its closure in 2012. (This sort of mixed-use programming was not unknown in the States; I used to frequent the three-screen Foxchase 3 in Alexandria, Virginia, which since the mid-seventies had been screening a combination of second-run arthouse movies and hardcore, and was demolished in 2005.)

Pornography has been a part of the private and public life of Taiwan since at least the sixties. Despite the KMT government's stringent regulation of porn – one of the targets of the party's Culture Purifying Movement – the first Danish, Dutch and Swedish smut found its way into Taipei cinemas at much the same time that it was taking the rest of the world by storm, followed in short order by a landfall of American adult films. The Yanks then dominated the Taiwanese market, abetted by a twelve-year ban on Japanese movies instated by the KMT, begun in 1972 in response to Japan's severing diplomatic relations with the ROC and establishing them with the PRC (the Japanese-ness of the cruising tourist in Tsai's film has a particular weight, given the fraught history between the two countries).

In porn, as in many things, little Taiwan found itself sandwiched between the influence of larger powers. By the eighties, Japanese AV (JAV), distinguished by its mosaicked genitalia and ingenious perversity, had gained a foothold through home video and broadcast on illegal cable television. In 1993, the KMT passed the Cable Radio and Television Law which legalised the use and broadcast of pornography in Taiwan. Still today, however, most Taiwanese talent gravitates to work in the bustling JAV industry – making the events of Tsai's next film, *The Wayward Cloud* (2005), in which Hsiao-kang becomes a porn performer, slightly unusual, if not impossible.

Goodbye, Dragon Inn is relatively chaste, at least as films concerned with cruising go, while *The Wayward Cloud* is quite explicit in its scenes of mechanistic rutting (at the time of writing, the film can be viewed in total at the porn-hosting site xvideos.com). A despairing facial money shot introduces one of *The Wayward Cloud*'s marvellous musical sequences, a barrelhouse blues number by Grace Chang mouthed by actress Yang Kuei-mei – but the release comes through the performance, not the final joyless, dutiful delivery of a gout of spooge.

Goodbye, Dragon Inn is a long, frottage-heavy tease without release, and as such makes an interesting counterpoint to Nolot's *Porn Theatre*, a film largely given over to matter-of-factly presenting the conventions of negotiating a mano a mano hook-up or group grope in the dark of a cinema. It is worth noting that the multi-hyphenate Nolot is the former lover of Roland Barthes, whose 'Leaving the Movie Theater', published in 1975 in the journal *Communications*, is one of the essential texts on the erotics of the cinema – and for Barthes, like the Tsai of *Goodbye, Dragon Inn*, 'cinema' connotes not only a medium, but a place: 'Whenever I hear the word *cinema*,' writes Barthes, 'I can't help thinking *hall*, rather than *film*.' He goes on:

> What does the 'darkness' of the cinema mean? ... Not only is the dark the very substance of reverie (in the pre-hypnoid meaning of the term); it is also the 'color' of a diffused eroticism; by its human condensation, by its absence of worldliness (contrary to the cultural *appearance* that has to be put in at any 'legitimate theater'), by the relaxation of postures (how many members of the cinema audience slide down into their seats as if into a bed, coats or feet thrown over the row in front!), the movie house (ordinary model) is a site of availability (even more than cruising), the inoccupation of bodies, which best defines modern eroticism – not that of advertising or striptease, but that of the big city. It is in this urban dark that the body's freedom is generated; this invisible work of possible affects emerges from a veritable cinematographic cocoon; the movie spectator could easily appropriate the silkworm's motto: *Inclusum labor illustrat*; it is because I am enclosed that I work and glow with all my desire.

The history of cruising at the cinema, it can be reasonably supposed, is as old as the medium itself. The hysterical reactions of matriarch

Amanda Wingfield to son Tom's nightly excursions to the movies in Tennessee Williams's 1944 *The Glass Menagerie* make quite a bit more sense when you consider that the memory play is the work of a gay man who'd spent his miserable mid-twenties working at the St. Louis factory of the International Shoe Company and concealing his furtive pleasures from the overbearing mother with whom he cohabited. (As in Williams's play, Tsai and Lee's earlier Hsiao-kang films are concerned with the practical exigencies of hiding one's sex life from the family with whom one shares a living space, a concealment which in *The River* flows towards a catastrophic confluence.)

A peerless account of the socio-sexual function of cinema buildings can be found in Samuel R. Delany's 1999 diptych of essays *Times Square Red, Times Square Blue*, which offers a first-hand autobiographical account of the author's regular visits to certain New York City movie theatres for same-sex encounters. The memoir section of the book covers a period of more than thirty years, beginning in the mid-sixties and ending with the Giuliani era "clean-up" achieved through the reworking of zoning laws, the crack-down vigilance of the Public Morals Squad and the swing of the wrecking ball, which vanished once thumping strips like the Deuce, the formerly cinema-clotted district on 42nd Street between 7th and 8th Avenues. Delany brings us inside a number of cinemas: the Eros I, Capri, and Venus, a trio of mini-theatres lining 45th Street to 8th Avenue; the Adonis on 51st Street, opened in 1921 as the Tivoli; and the Variety Photoplays on Third Avenue between 13th and 14th Streets, immortalised in Scorsese's *Taxi Driver* (1976) and *Variety*. All are now gone. The Eros has become the Playwright Celtic Pub. The Adonis was demolished in 1995, replaced three years later by a 26-storey apartment building. The Variety Photoplays is now a glass box condominium; the theatre closed in 2004 and was torn down the following year.

What Delany is eulogising is not only these physical theatres or the films they showed – though he has much to say on both subjects – but instead the entire culture of the casual public encounter, in this case a sexual one, that their existence facilitated. This, too, is part of what Tsai's movie bids goodbye to – the beacon brightness of the neighbourhood theatres that welcomed flocks, as well as their touching final acts, in which they became smouldering havens for a few stragglers looking for a casual caress.

In his analysis of the 'metacinematic cruising' in Tsai's film, scholar Nicholas de Villiers notes how the positioning of the Japanese tourist's search for sex against the backdrop of Hu's wuxia classic proposes a counterpoint between two kinds of random encounters. Tsai's films, per de Villiers, place the issue of desire at the forefront and are distinctly modern and urban in character, revolving around the sort of chance encounters that a tightly packed city encourages – take for example *The River*, the events of which are set in motion when Chen catches sight of Lee as they pass one another on escalators headed in opposite directions. Hu's film, by contrast, represents the landscape of rural inns and countryside highways of the 'classical novel or *wuxia pian* cinematic narrative', in which homoeroticism, if perhaps present on some level, doesn't find overt expression.

The wuxia – the word is commonly translated as 'martial heroes', and sometimes as synonymous with 'martial arts' – is both ancient and relatively new, like so much in the popular culture of Greater China. Wuxia stories centre on heroic *xia* warriors, and the scholar Sam Ho draws out an effective definition of the genre in its very name:

> The Chinese word *wu* is written by combining two other characters, *zhi* and *ge*, meaning 'stop' and 'fight', respectively. In other words, the term is an oxymoron, suggesting that it takes fighting to put an end to fighting, a paradox that is central to the appeal of the *wuxia* form. The term *xia*, however, has nothing at all in common with the English 'arts'. It can be loosely translated as 'chivalrous hero', although that meaning incorporates connotations that have accumulated over time.

In literary form, wuxia can be dated back to the ninth century, in the later Tang Dynasty. The Ming period produced much-cited classics – *Water Margin* and *The Romance of Three Kingdoms* – but it wasn't until the early years of the ROC that the modern wuxia novel appeared, published in serial form in newspapers that sought to secure the services of popular writers in their circulation wars. Films followed: Tianyi, a Shanghai studio operated by the Shaw brothers, later of Hong Kong, made one of the first known wuxia films, *Swordswoman Li Feifei*, in 1925. The production of wuxia in China would eventually be barred by the relentlessly modernising KMT, who deemed the genre retrograde and encouraging of superstition, but the movies never wholly disappeared between then and their breakout moment in the mid-sixties, their production having largely decamped to wide open Hong Kong and other sites.

As a "national" genre, the wuxia has most often been likened to the American western and the Japanese *chambara*, or samurai film. Like the western and samurai hero, the wuxia hero is guided by a personal code, though unlike the samurai, they typically stand outside of, and are often placed in direct conflict with, the aristocratic power structure. Pertinent to Tsai's cinema – and here is the connection that de Villiers draws out – the wuxia hero is a wayfaring stranger, travelling the countryside of an ancient China that as often as not is being terrorised by its leaders, righting wrongs through martial mastery. Tsai, too, focuses on wanderers through hostile environments, though his chosen landscape is the depredated modern city terrorised, in a less direct and heavy-handed manner, by its leaders – not scheming eunuchs, but rather an eternally rebuilding local government and the larger forces of global capital, from the mandates of which no locality can be sovereign. This ongoing process of head-first, ravenous change, and in particular the continual destruction and reshaping of the city that goes on with little regard to servicing the needs of any but its richest residents, is felt throughout Tsai's cinema. Tsai's 1991 telefilm *Give Me a Home* and his 2006 *I Don't Want to Sleep Alone*, for example, portray the difficulties of construction workers and labourers who toil to alter the urban landscape while standing to benefit in no way from the changes.

His proclivity for dramatising urban peregrinations have led many to compare Tsai, particularly early in his career, to Antonioni, though Tsai is individuated by, if nothing else, his sense of humour, a characteristic Antonioni can't be said to have had in overabundance. Tsai's films are undeniably suffused with the pain of alone-in-the-crowd urbanity, and in this belong to a rich strain of Taiwanese filmmaking: not for nothing did Hou pick the title *A City of Sadness*. Time and again in Tsai's films the metropolis is seen as a place that breeds isolation and loneliness. But if city life is a sickness, through holding forth the potential for contact it also contains the possibility of its own cure.

'Antonioniesque' is often used as a shorthand for any film dealing with alienated wandering and urban anomie, though the concept of the flâneur observer predates the beginning of the Italian's career by a century or so, its legacy running through Baudelaire to the Walter Benjamin of *The Arcades Project* – which could be an alternate title for *Rebels of the Neon God*, with its time-capsule record of the video game parlours of Ximending, before the extensive public works that would transform the area into a bright, carnivalesque pedestrian district modelled after Tokyo's Harajuku. For Baudelaire, writing in 'The Painter of Modern Life', the ambulatory gaze of the flâneur seeks 'to extract from fashion whatever element it may contain of poetry within history, to distil the eternal from the transitory.' While Tsai's camera does something akin to this for Taipei, Paris, Kuala Lumpur in *I Don't Want to Sleep Alone* and Bangkok in *Days*, his characters are usually obeying more protean, and often romantic/erotic drives.

In his *The Flâneur: A Stroll Through the Paradoxes of Paris*, the writer Edmund White connects the figure of the flâneur – 'that aimless stroller who loses himself in the crowd, who has no destination and goes wherever caprice or curiosity directs his or her steps' – to the act of cruising, proclaiming, 'To be gay and cruise is perhaps an extension of the flâneur's very essence, or at least its most successful application.' Something in the French character seems to lend itself to the cinematic depiction of the act of cruising; the last twenty years have not only given us Nolot's *Porn Theatre*, but also Alain Guiraudie's *Stranger by the Lake* (2013) and José Luis Guerín's *In the City of Sylvia* (2007), which tracks the movement of a heterosexual male's wandering eye through the streets of Strasbourg. (Wilson notes that while the English 'cruise' has a strictly gay connotation, the French *draguer* is also heterosexual.)

Baudelaire's flâneur of the 1860s wandered a Paris unrecognisable from what it had been ten years previous, and to be rendered unrecognisable again ten years hence, a city in the midst of the seventeen-year process of Haussmannisation – the massive public works programme initiated by Emperor Napoléon III and spearheaded by his prefect of Seine, Georges-Eugène Haussmann, which turned the knotty, dark, cluttered medieval city into the metropolis of broad boulevards we know today. Today, in most every major city in the world, from Ximending to Times Square, a new sort of Haussmannisation is and has been underway, one of its models the process of redevelopment that Delany describes.

Delany's project was born of years observing the changing face of the city around him, an awareness of which is one of the side effects of growing older. On his early forays into Times Square, he writes, 'Like many young people, I'd assumed the world – the physical reality of stores, restaurant locations, apartment buildings, and movie theaters and the kinds of people who lived in this or that neighbourhood – was far more stable than it was.' Kent Jones, in a not wholly dissimilar vein, comments on awakening from this illusion of continuity in cinema at the dawn of the twenty-first century, for 'through the nineties, "The Movies" was a common reference point, as apparently solid as the Grand Canyon.' It was the first glimmer of this impermanence of things, I believe, that I experienced in 1997 at the Tri-County 1–5.

With the passage of time, the transitory, mutable nature of a cityscape – or an art form – becomes more and more evident. If you stay in a city long enough, it becomes populated by the ghosts of storefronts past – the restaurants that are now Chase banks, the Dunkin' Donuts that used to be a bar where you once puked in the bathroom sink, the storefronts and cinemas standing empty while neighbourhoods are made ghost towns by the prohibitively expensive demands of landlords. This consciousness of change was central to Antonioni and several of his Italian contemporaries, whose films captured the concrete fever of the Italian economic miracle – *il boom* – and it is essential, too, to Tsai.

'Our cities are changing all the time,' he has said. 'It is as if we are living in a giant building site. I never avoid these places in my films. They remind us of what we are losing. They have an emotional appeal, as if they are characters themselves with their own stories to tell.'

5.

The story to be told in *Goodbye, Dragon Inn* is that of the Fu-Ho Grand itself, the theatre the transitory element made eternal – a once vital feature of the urban landscape, now a refuge for nostalgists retreating into their memories and a stage for what appear to be largely anonymous sexual encounters, a repository of living history soon to be shuttered for good. By breaking from the screen to scrutinise the cinema hall in the opening scene, Tsai practices the 'another way of going to the movies' described by Barthes:

> letting oneself be fascinated *twice over*, by the image and its surroundings – as if I had two bodies at the same time: a narcissistic body which gazes, lost, into the engulfing mirror, and a perverse body, ready to fetishize not the image

> but precisely what exceeds it: the texture of the sound, the hall, the darkness, the obscure mass of the other bodies, the rays of light, entering the theater, leaving the hall.

The recurring presence of the Fu-Ho signifies something that had become increasingly prevalent in Tsai's work around this time, an exploration of the subject of the cinema itself – again, both the medium and the physical place, another of the public urban spaces that Tsai gravitates towards.

While Tsai's first two theatrical features do not explicitly address the role of films and filmgoing in their characters' lives – in *Rebels of the Neon God*, the most prominent cinematic point of reference is the James Dean poster that graces the arcade's wall – it's with *The River*, Tsai's third feature, that a pronounced metacinematic element begins to filter in. The movie's key meeting ground is another cruising spot, a gay bathhouse rife with possibilities for the random encounter, but its sparse plot is set in motion by an encounter with the filmmaking process. Hsiao-kang, on bumping into an ex-girlfriend, tags along to a movie shoot she's working on, and is recruited to play a corpse floating face down in the polluted Tamsui River after the mannequin being used for the job has proven unsatisfactory – a scene echoing one in *All Corners of the World*, in which a mannequin spotted floating in the surf is mistaken for a dead body. The part of the director is played by Ann Hui, Tsai's friend and perhaps the most acclaimed of the filmmakers affiliated with the first generation of the Hong Kong New Wave, and her amiably strong-arming a reluctant Hsiao-kang into bobbing in the sludgy water is a discomfortingly funny study in directorial soft power persuasion. (Lee would appear two years later in Hui's *Ordinary Heroes*, one of his occasional forays away from Tsai's cinema.)

As it happens, Hsiao-kang is right to be reluctant; after filming his brief, anonymous part, he develops a kink in his neck that leans his head to one side, accompanied by a persistent twitch. (The inspiration comes from life, specifically Lee being stricken by a mysterious neck ailment after the shooting of *Rebels of the Neon God*, the same lingering malady that still persists in *Days*.) The cinema, here, is dangerous, an agent of destruction, of infection. In *The River*, moving images are both a source of contamination and a source of distracted, despondent contemplation: Hsiao-kang's mother is carrying on a desultory affair with a porno vendor, but seems to derive more pleasure and emotional connection from the JAV videos she is seen watching, both alone and in his company, than from the time they pass together, which is marked by a boredom fringing onto antipathy.

Goodbye, Dragon Inn, by comparison, is less bitter than bittersweet. On a subconscious level at least, the idea of revisiting the cinemas of his youth had been on Tsai's mind for some time. 'When I began to make films, I started to have a recurring dream about a cinema called the Odeon, and I had it often until I was 40 years old,' he wrote. 'I didn't understand it at all. It didn't occur to me in my everyday thoughts and yet it presented itself to me each night. Perhaps, I thought, it meant that I was getting old?'

In the same piece from 2016, Tsai described returning to Kuching to find the cinemas of his boyhood 'demolished, except one, which no longer showed film. It had become a market for various knickknacks. I saw very clearly then that I came into this world at a time of unprecedented rapid change.' The cinema in question is almost certainly the Cathay, which Lau writes of in its present state as 'nestled rather insalubriously among rusting warehouses and a clutch of crumbling shophouses. It's currently occupied by a chain store selling bulk souvenirs.' There are still screens aplenty in Kuching today, but what has disappeared are the big single-screen houses, whose dying off Lau goes on to recount. Their reign, he writes,

> ended swiftly with the advent of the shopping mall and the cineplex. These behemoths gobbled up the older icons of town life and trapped them inside large windowless boxes. Gone were the hawker stalls, the easy connections to the street, the fantastical architecture. In the new age of mass consumption and the ubiquitous car, there was no longer a place for these familiar touchstones. We exchanged them for convenient parking, air-conditioned corridors, and a choice of popcorn sets.

The process he discusses, though occurring perhaps a few years later, is much the same one that decimated the American movie palaces during the urban renewal period of the sixties and seventies. The big houses that weren't pulled down outright were vivisected for multiplexing while, outside of the cities proper, suburban 'plexes sprouted like toadstools in the middle of vast parking lots – self-contained island cinema-cities with no easy connections to the street, indeed, no street to speak of at all. It was during this period that the Tri-County where I saw *Spawn* was built, the advert for the grand opening on 11 July 1975 boasting, 'With a trio of screens from which to choose, the odds in favour of your finding the best in film entertainment are now 3 to 1.'

The Tri-County cinema, which expanded eventually to five screens and in time also operated the two screens of the former Princeton Cinemas 1 & 2 nearby, was an architecturally undistinguished bunker house building of which I was nevertheless fond, connected as it was to many of my earliest filmgoing memories: the 1983 theatrical re-release of *Snow White and the Seven*

Dwarfs (1937), which my mother had to carry me out of to quell my incessant wailing; a 1987 showing of *Jaws: The Revenge*, during which my mother had to squire my friend Ben Ritchey out to the lobby after he lost it at the scene of Mitchell Anderson having his arm ripped off in the first reel; and several other movies that progressed without any noteworthy panic attacks or babysitting demands on my mother. As cinematic experiences, mine might not measure up to what Tsai would have seen as a boy – he has written of being dumbstruck by the image of 'a brilliant carp spirit who has taken on the form of a beautiful woman emerging from a pond, vividly glistening, dazzling and unforgettable' from Ying Yunwei's 1959 *Chasing the Fish Spirit* – but nostalgia of this sort is indifferent to such distinctions. We have no choice of what we consume or where we consume it; it is enough that it was *our* experience, *our* youth.

This point is understood in the short Tsai made between *What Time Is It There?* and *Goodbye, Dragon Inn*, titled *The Skywalk Is Gone* (2002).

It's a sequel of sorts to the feature that precedes it, in the sense that all of the Hsiao-kang films can be read as sequels to one another – to those inclined, they might be viewed as an ongoing epic of sustained character development, like that undertaken by Jean-Pierre Léaud as Antoine Doinel in the cycle of films beginning with *The 400 Blows* (1959) that Truffaut made featuring his alter ego character.

In *The Skywalk Is Gone*, Chen's character, back from Paris, returns to seek out Hsiao-kang at the site of the Taipei Train Station overpass where he'd had his watch-selling concession, and where they shared their brief moments together. After a series of long takes that illustrate her extreme discombobulation when faced with a city so recently departed and now so profoundly altered, she discovers that the skywalk has been demolished without a trace, replaced by an underpass allowing for pedestrian traffic beneath the busy throughway. In this unrecognisable landscape, Hsiao-kang is nowhere to be found. (He is eventually seen auditioning for a role in a porno, working his way into the vocation he occupies in

The Wayward Cloud, and indeed wearing a doctor's outfit, as he is in the beginning of that film.)

Separating pedestrian traffic from that of cars below, the skywalk is a little-loved "innovation" that belongs to sixties urban planning and redevelopment at its most destructive and antihuman, connoting a surrendering of the street level to the encroachments of its noisy new ruler, the automobile. In the American city, at least, skywalks were also associated with cold weather climes and, unofficially, white flight and mounting anxiety surrounding urban centres, providing a means for the suburban businessman to move between office towers without being jostled by panhandlers or otherwise soiled by contact with the hoi polloi. In Tsai's film, however, the disappearance of the skywalk doesn't signify a change for the better. The pedestrian who doesn't opt to scuttle underground can't cross the street without risk to life and limb or, as we see, a ticket from an over-vigilant police officer.

The skywalk belongs to the category of landmarks within the corporate culture-moulded landscape that the anthropologist Marc Augé termed 'non-places'. These architectural manifestations of hypermodern existence, liminal sites through which one passes in transit, include shopping malls, supermarkets, hotels and motels, airports, superhighways, food courts and convenience stores – all backdrops, it should be noted, against which a goodly portion of Tsai's films are seen to play out. Taipei and Hong Kong, modern cities grown overnight to metropolis-size at mid-century by an influx of refugees, are perhaps the definitive non-place cities of the twentieth century, and as such ideal bellwethers to understanding the changing cultural constructions of public space in a world increasingly given over to non-spaces. (In the twenty-first century they may have been outstripped by the aggressively remade Mainland megalopolises from Chengdu to Dalian, each now topped out by a smattering of indistinguishable starchitect skyscrapers.)

To mourn the exalted memory of a cinema is one thing, but to homage the memory of a skywalk is quite another. Walking through the precincts of waterfront north Brooklyn recently, I thought of all the newly ubiquitous and inevitably doomed business models that had cropped up in the last fifteen years, as online shopping closed down walk-in shops and storefronts offering place-specific, experiential inducements proliferated. Soon they, too, might be eulogised: The CBD Dispensary is Gone. The WeWork is Gone. The Urban Climbing Gym is Gone. The Escape Room is Gone. The Team-Building Axe Throwing Range is Gone. And yet, no less than my homely suburban multiplex, the unlovely skywalk can function as a repository of memory, a space where lives can intersect, and be changed for that intersection. The skywalk, too, can be missed when it is gone.

Against the non-place, Augé proposes the 'place', defined as locations

> of identity, of relations and of history. The layout of the house, the rules of residence, the zoning of the village, placement of altars, con figuration of public open spaces, land distribution, correspond for every individual to a system of possibilities, prescriptions and interdicts whose content is both spatial and social.

This notion might be extended to apply to that altar of entertainment, the neighbourhood cinema – recall Alan Lau's use of 'secular temples' when describing the cinemas of Kuching. This linkage between cinema and church is hardly novel, made explicit in *The Long Day Closes* (1992), perhaps the supreme work by an artist who resembles Tsai not a little in his nostalgia and his wrestling with the deceptions of nostalgia, Terence Davies. Illustrating the principal institutions shaping his young protagonist and alter ego, Bud, Davies lap dissolves between an overhead shot of a movie house audience and a church congregation observing High Mass.

In playing witness to the last gasp of the neighbourhood theatre of the sort familiar from his youth, is Tsai tracking the journey of the cinema from place to non-place? From secular temple to the exurban multiplex, its screens given over to those 'wholly interchangeable slabs of worldwide entertainment' described by Jones?

6.

Cinema construction, along with construction in general, exploded in Taiwan in the years after it was returned to ROC rule. Taiwan saw its population more than double between 1940 and 1966, and with this infusion of raw, teeming humanity came a furious flurry of building activity accompanying the so-called Taiwan Economic Miracle, the fast-forward industrialisation of the island nation with the assistance of US financial aid. Movie palaces were erected and Ximending, Taipei's theatre district, was alight with the neon of new cinemas. The boom in theatre building was by no means limited to the cities, nor was the grandeur of the constructions: in the little town of Guānshān, the 1,200-seat Zhōnghuá

Theatre rose, nicknamed the 'northern tyrant' for its bulk.

Ten years Tsai's senior, Edward Yang grew up in Taipei in the fifties and sixties, and would describe both the prevalence of 'Mandarin films from Hong Kong' and the cosmopolitan film culture of the city of his youth:

> It was only after I got much older that I started to wonder how it was that I came to have seen so many European and Japanese art films. I thought about it and realized I had seen them all in my childhood during that era. At that time, the Republic of China had official diplomatic relations with most of the major Western countries in the world, and one thing that they did in order to curry favor with these nations was to release their films. *(Laughs.)* So in the busy district of Ximending where all the movie theaters were, there were two theaters that played only Italian films, two theaters that played French films, another few theaters that played Japanese films; so there was an incredible selection of films to choose from. We would see films like Fellini's *8 ½* (1963) during their commercial release run

> in Taipei as children! My French friends were shocked when I told them that Robert Bresson's films had been commercially released in Taipei.

And there was the local industry, as well. Cinema was introduced to Taiwan at the beginning of Japanese rule by coloniser Takamatsu Toyojirō, who as an independent filmmaker made works catering to the audiences back home, titles like *Conquering Taiwan's Native Rebels* (1910) giving some sense of their content. During Japanese subjecthood, Taiwan never emerged as a major production centre – its output was nowhere near that of Japan or, say, Japanese-occupied Manchuria, where in the thirties and forties the Manchukuo Film Association made a star out of China-raised, Mandarin-fluent, ethnically Japanese actress Yoshiko 'Shirley' Yamaguchi, renamed Li Xianglan in order to conceal her origins. (In 1943's *Bell of Sayon*, Yamaguchi plays an aboriginal Taiwanese.)

In parallel with the upswing in cinema construction in Taiwan that followed the ROC's skittled return, a new film industry developed, largely operated under the oversight of various ruling factions. Patriotic propaganda, newsreels and educational shorts were made through the military; narrative films were produced by the KMT, through a subsidiary none too alluringly called the Farming and Education Film Company; documentaries and narrative films dedicated to conveying positive social messages were produced by the Taiwan Film Culture Company, under the provisional government, which was distinct from the KMT. (Both the Mainlanders and the Taiwanese regard Taiwan as a province of China, not a nation unto itself. The agreement ends there.) When these companies joined forces in 1954, creating the Central Motion Picture Corporation (CMPC), production of anti-communist melodramas started in bulk – though largely in the local dialect of Taiwanese Hokkien, both language and subject matter limiting their potential for export.

Taiwan was an important market for Hong Kong films from the fifties on, but the sixties saw significant development of a Taiwanese popular cinema. A key figure in this bustling period – perhaps *the* key figure – was none other than the director of *Dragon Inn*, King Hu.

Born in 1932 in Beijing, Hu obtained a travel permit to the city of Hong Kong after the PLA carried the day in '49, and arrived there at age eighteen, finding work as an infamously meticulous proofreader, movie billboard painter and then a set decorator at Great Wall Motion Picture Company. Shortly the young Hu would move into acting, debuting as a rowdy teenager in Yen Chun's *Laughter and Tears* (produced in 1953–4 but delayed in release until '58), after he was recommended for the part by screenwriter/assistant director Li Han-hsiang, whom he'd befriended at Great Wall, and who would become a mentor of sorts, as well as one of the pre-eminent Shaw directors of the fifties and early sixties.

Hu continued to perform through the fifties – the same years when Run Run Shaw, an aggressive businessman and micromanaging control freak who'd come to town fresh from Singapore, was establishing himself as a force in the suddenly crowded and lucrative industry, building a 46-acre studio complex in which to base the operations of Shaw Brothers Ltd. Shaw's Movietown was a satellite city unto itself, an undertaking on a scale heretofore unseen in Hong Kong, boasting twelve sound stages, thirty outdoor stages, dormitories for 1,200 workers and apartments for stars and directors, who were trained and cultivated in-house and signed to demanding contracts, as in the old Hollywood studio system that was then well on its way to unravelling. By the end of the fifties, Shaw Brothers were rivalled in power in Hong Kong only by the Cathay Organisation, and after Cathay head and founder Dato Loke Wan Tho's death in a 1964 plane crash, they reigned supreme.

Hu eventually went to work for Shaw Brothers, appearing before Li's camera in *The Kingdom and the Beauty* (1959), among other projects. All the while, Hu was campaigning to launch himself as a filmmaker, and served as the assistant director to Li on the the *huangmei diao* (Yellow Plum opera) classic *The Love Eterne* (1963). The film was a sensation, especially in Taiwan – per scholar Ramona Curry, 'an unprecedented cultural phenomenon that critics have characterized as a craze and a frenzy.' Its success allowed Li to strike out on his own, heading to Taiwan to set up, with financial assistance from Shaw rival MPGI, his own production company far away from the domain of the Shaw Brothers organisation. (Expressions of feeling stifled by the hands-on, meddlesome Run Run are found throughout a number of recollections of the period.) In the years following Li's departure, Hu, fighting with his employer all the way, finally established himself as a director.

Run Run, who had nurtured a soft spot for the wuxia pian since the Shaws turned out *Swordswoman Li Feifei* when he was but a neophyte businessman of eighteen, had conspired to effectively relaunch the genre. In 1965, the official Shaw magazine *Southern Screen* published an article boasting of a forthcoming 'color wuxia offensive', in which 'Shaws will break with tradition ... Creating a new vista for martial arts films. The fake, fantastical, and theatrical fighting and the so-called special effects of the past will be replaced by realistic action and fighting that immediately decides life or death.'

The first films of this colour offensive, Hsu Tseng-hung's *Temple of the Red Lotus* and *The Twin Swords*, made little impact on the public when released in 1965, but two films released in the second wave did: Chang Cheh's *The One-Armed Swordsman* (1967), the first movie in Hong Kong history to earn HK$1M at the box office, and Hu's *Come Drink With Me* (1966) – a massive hit starring Shaw contract players Yue Hua, Chen Hung-lieh and Cheng Pei-pei, whose performance as heroine Golden Swallow vaulted her into the ranks of celebrity.

Come Drink With Me redefined and reinvigorated the wuxia pian, helping to bring a nimble new visual vocabulary, blood-red violence, and grounding historical detail in the production design to what previously had been considered a somewhat disreputable, cheapjack genre, associated with fifties Wong Fei-hung films starring Kwan Tak-hing and early sixties low-budget Cantonese serials. Its success earned Hu a four-film contract offer from Taiwan's Union Film Company, which Hu, tired of clashing with Run Run, happily signed, following his old friend Li into exodus. (Run Run's deputy, Raymond Chow, meanwhile flew out to Taipei to hardball negotiate the foreign distribution rights for Hu's next four films, meaning Hu wasn't free of the Shaws yet. When Tsai saw *Dragon Inn* in Kuching, then, it was likely at the Shaw-aligned Capitol.)

This stream of defections – Li, Hu and, eventually, *One-Armed Swordsman* star Jimmy Wang Yu – as well as the maturation of local talent like director Li Hsing, signalled a major advancement for Taiwanese cinema. Following the even bigger success throughout Southeast Asia of *Dragon Inn*, Union Film (alongside China Arts Motion Picture Company and International Film Company) broke ground on what was to become the largest privately owned studio in Taipei, the International Motion Picture Studio, which began full-steam-ahead production of wuxia.

The late sixties would be the busiest years in the history of Taiwanese cinema; in 1969, the industry produced 230 films, its all-time record. Even in these years, however, local product faced stiff competition from Hong Kong imports at the box office, and in the decades to come Hong Kong established its dominance of (and dependence on) the Taipei market. It was Hong Kong, not Taipei, that had become and would remain the moviemaking capitol of Greater China, inheritor of the mantle surrendered by Shanghai, whose entertainment professionals in large part headed south after '49 – a migration suggested by the end of Tsui Hark's period piece *Shanghai Blues* (1984), in which nightclub performers played by singer Kenny Bee and Sylvia Chang hop the last train out of Shanghai for a future down south.

While never exactly fighting on even footing with the Hong Kong industry, Taiwanese cinema enjoyed a *succès d'estime* in the eighties with a sharp rise in international profile. The CMPC studio under producer Ming Chi put its support behind filmmakers like Yang and Hou, who would become the breakout figures of what came to be packaged as the Taiwanese New Wave, following on the heels of Hong Kong's, whose central figures included Hui and Tsui. While the Hong Kong New Wavers routinely worked in pop idioms, the Taiwanese were making films of a more contemplative ilk, increasingly sombre and austere.[1] It was Ming's successor, Xu Ligong, who would help to get Tsai's career off the ground, helping him take his place in the so-called Second Wave – but by the time the younger director began his feature filmmaking endeavours in the nineties, the local film industry in his adopted home was facing a crisis.

Along with incursions by Hollywood product, the spread of piracy had gouged deeply into profits. This had devastating results for Taiwanese filmmakers – and also for the Hong Kong industry, already collapsing under an insupportable burden of overproduction and high-strung over the impending 1997 Handover that would join the port city to Mainland China as a Special Administrative Unit under fifty years of 'One country, two systems' rule. As the receipts coming back looked mingier and mingier, everything fell to pieces.

Two prominent deaths would make the shaky state of the Taiwanese industry's health particularly palpable. While shooting a historical drama for television in Beijing, Li Han-hsiang, Hu's friend and mentor, died of a heart attack in December 1996. Hu had enjoyed popularity and critical esteem beyond that of any martial arts filmmaker before him – his 1971 *A Touch of Zen*, proselytised for by influential critic and tastemaker Pierre Rissient, received a prize at Cannes in 1975, a first for a wuxia – but his own career had fared badly since the late seventies in the absence of box office hits. He had finally, however, been seeing some forward momentum for his own decades-in-the-making historical epic, *The Battle of Ono*, which was to concern nineteenth-century Chinese railroad labourers in the American West. With such a grand undertaking before him, Hu grew suddenly anxious about his own health and went for a check-up while in Taiwan to attend Li's memorial service. The results were unhappy. Submitting to a recommended angioplasty, Hu suffered a stroke when a blood clot travelled to his brain, and he died, aged 64, on 14 January 1997. Per his *The Battle of Ono* producing partner Sarah Pillsbury, Hu at the end of his life had been in a eulogistic mode: 'Before King Hu left Los Angeles to pay tribute to Li Han-hsiang, he was lamenting the loss of the old generation of craftsmen.'

Tsai, on hearing the news, would have been preparing *The River* for its Berlin premiere. The fact of Hu's death, and the dire straits of Taiwan's popular cinema – with production dropping to less than twenty films that year – must have sent Tsai into some lamentations of his own. All of this would have been very much on his mind when he conceived of *Goodbye, Dragon Inn*, an idea that began with the foundering Fu-Ho Grand.

Located on the fringe of the neighbourhood where Tsai was then living, Yonghe in New Taipei, the Fu-Ho Grand was discovered during the making of *What Time Is It There?*, one of those bits of location scouting luck out of which his cinema, so concerned with chance encounters, often seems to naturally evolve – the discovery of loitering arcade rat Lee, or the stumbling across the mural by artist Kao Jun-Honn that concludes his *Stray Dogs* (2013), likewise a piece of fortunate happenstance. 'I found an old cinema on the outskirts of Taipei where I wanted to shoot,' Tsai recounted of finding the Fu-Ho.

> The feeling of being there had a flavor of death and fecundity, as though I were meeting an old lost friend. Afterwards, I chose this dilapidated old theater – perpetually on the verge of

> bankruptcy – as the venue for my premiere. It was a dark and stormy night, but the theater was packed. The next day the theater manager called to ask if I would enter into a partnership with him. Of course I turned down this terrible business proposal. He said to me, 'Then I have no option but to close the cinema.' I responded, 'Wait a minute, okay, rent it to me for one year.' During the subsequent year, I made *Goodbye, Dragon Inn*.

Opened in 1972 – five years too late for a first run of *Dragon Inn* – and out of business thirty years later, the 1,000-seat, single-screen Fu-Ho Grand was at the time of its ribbon cutting the largest cinema in Taipei County, part of an innovative mixed-use complex including a traditional market, space for stalls and shops on its second floor and apartment blocks on its upper floors. (To the massive Fu Hall, seen in Tsai's film, a 200-seat Hu Hall, not shown, was later added.)

Across Taiwan, many of these constructions have since been pulled down or repurposed. One, the Dōngxìng Theatre in the southern Huādōng Valley, has become a rural hospital. Others moulder in ruins, like the Xiluo Theatre, abandoned in 1988, a concrete and brick structure erected over a wooden cinema built sometime in the twenties, or the Keelung Dàhuá Theatre, which has stood silent for decades on the edge of the port town of Keelung City's red-light district. Many were carved up, like the Ambassador in Taipei, whose 1,500-seat hall became three theatres. A handful continue to function, like the seventy-year-old Chuang Mei Theatre in Tainan; known for its hand-painted movie posters, the venue was frequented by a young Ang Lee in his student days.

At the end of its life, the Fu-Ho was playing second-run films on double bills. The building still stands today, cost prohibitive to renovate, impossible to demolish due to the nature of the structure that it's a part of, an urban relic that the local homeless, it's said, would rather sleep rough than pass a night inside of. 'Did you know this theatre is haunted?'

Goodbye, Dragon Inn was initially imagined as part of a diptych film, a *moyen métrage* of about an hour's length, to be paired with a work of approximately the same runtime, Lee's directorial debut. Recalled Lee: 'We had just finished filming *What Time Is It There?* and Tsai wanted to continue certain motives and locales of that movie, especially "the cinema" ... Tsai's film became too long so we decided to lengthen my film as well so we could have two separate films.' And so two long shorts became two stand-alone features, Tsai's *Goodbye, Dragon Inn* and Lee's *The Missing* (2003), which follows two pairs of accidentally separated relations. Distributed individually, the finished films remain, per Lee, united by certain thematic affinities: 'Tsai's film is about the vanishing of these old-style cinemas in Taiwan, my film deals with the disappearance of interpersonal communication.'

And for Tsai, there is a tangible connection between the old-style cinema and interpersonal communication. The single-screen cinema, of the sort Tsai grew up inside, is a physical manifestation and memento of a more unified communal pop culture – or monoculture – that by the turn of the century had effectively ceased to exist. It offered a single option, in many cases servicing a contiguous neighbourhood in the manner of a local grocer or hairdresser or noodle shop – and so people who lived together would enter the cinema to have the same dream together, the quality of that dream, or lack thereof, arbitrarily determined by the negotiations between distributor and exhibitor.

The multiplex, a phenomenon in many cases concomitant to increasing suburban sprawl, was one step towards the fragmentation of the audience and a separation of the cinema from the life of the street; it would be carried still further by home video's market saturation, as VCRs made every parlour into a theatre. The social space of the cinema lost ground to the private space of television, and with this went a powerful incubator of fantasy. Barthes compares the alluring 'darkness of the cinema' with its electric potential, its anonymity, its eroticism, to the domestic familiarity of TV, writing that 'television *doomed* us to the Family, whose household instrument it has become – what the hearth used to be, flanked by its communal kettle.' Originator of the idea of the non-place, Augé concurs in his slim book on *Casablanca* (1942): 'Cinema must remain the occasion of a meeting or encounter. That is [one] reason why I am not a lover of DVDs.'

Other factors were in play in Taiwan, by the early nineties the largest market in Southeast Asia for the home video industry, where the old movie houses were rapidly losing eyeballs to MTV – not the music television channel, but the name given to rooms rented out for videotape viewing. In Taipei alone one concern, Solar Systems, ran a chain with one hundred rental spaces across the city, where patrons could choose from over twenty-five thousand titles, paying NT$160 per person for admission. (A ticket to the cinema, by comparison, would've run in the area of NT$225, or US$7.) Pirate stations piped into Taiwanese homes, the Channel 4s – so called because they existed outside of the three legal broadcast channels – were another popular phenomenon detracting from cinema box office, as many as seven hundred of them in business at the same time. (On the Channel 4s, JAV was to be found aplenty.) Video rental and sale shops abounded, many or even most of them trafficking in pirated goods; a 1990 study estimated that almost a third of Taiwan's video shops operated outside the law, though a 1992 *Billboard* piece suggests locals put the number two to three times higher.

One of these pirate video vendors makes an appearance in *What Time Is It There?* – a sidewalk shop specialising in classics where Hsiao-kang goes looking for a French film that will show him Paris, and comes home with a copy of Truffaut's autobiographical debut *The 400 Blows*. In that film, Truffaut relives his truant adolescence; in one larcenous interlude, we see Antoine Doinel (Léaud) and his friend René (Patrick Auffay) steal a photograph of the busty actress Gianna Maria Canale as she appears in the 1954 Italian film *Theodora, Slave Empress*. Just as Truffaut would later boast, 'I saw my first two hundred films on the sly, playing hooky and slipping into the movie houses without paying,' in *Mes petites amoureuses* Eustache goes so far as to give a primer on how to sneak into the cinema, while in *All Corners of the World*, Tsai presents cinema and petty thievery as practically synonymous. In an early scene, the family's youngest child and a gaggle of friends rush past a ticket taker to catch a free show of what appears to be a Category III-type sex film titled *The Lady and the Gardener*. Later, the family of scalpers, called 'yellow cows' in Chinese slang, discuss the profitability of various films, with star vehicles for Jackie Chan and Arnold Schwarzenegger mentioned in the unlikely company of Hou's *A City of Sadness*.

A few years on, the yellow cows of *All Corners of the World* would've probably moved on to greener pastures, setting up a tape stall if they'd hoped to stay in business. The bootleg shop in *What Time Is It There?* represents another generation's method of seeing movies on the sly, a new distribution system that had potential to do much to democratise cinema, even as it would devastate its practical profitability, the very means of its existence.

1 The Hong Kongers' work was often infused with a pop sensibility. Ann Hui followed her dark, atmospheric theatrical debut *The Secret* (1979) with a horror-comedy called *The Spooky Bunch* (1980) starring Kenny Bee. Hou Hsiao-hsien's first films were lightweight affairs made with Bee – *Cute Girl* (1980), *Cheerful Wind* (1981) and *The Green, Green Grass of Home* (1982) – but the films that he would go on to make after beginning his collaboration with screenwriter Chu T'ien-wen were more contemplative, as was Edward Yang's watershed *Taipei Story* (1985), co-written by Yang, Chu and Hou, who also stars.

7.

Truffaut was among the European directors that Tsai had first encountered as a student, seeing *The Story of Adele H.* (1975) early, then seeking out the rest of the Frenchman's filmography. Explaining Truffaut's appeal, Tsai said: 'He has created his own world, which he films again and again. He always has the same preoccupations that find their way back into his films. And I like that very much.' The impact of the Doinel cycle on Tsai cannot be overstated – indeed, Léaud himself appears in both of Tsai's Paris-set films, *What Time Is It There?* and *Face* (2009), another metacinematic exercise which finds Lee playing a Taiwanese filmmaker shooting a film in the environs of the Louvre.

Regarding his own decades-spanning dedication to filming Lee, Tsai has cited the precedent of Truffaut's relationship with Léaud:

> There is something very unique about film: its reality is not the same as the reality of real life. However, you cannot say the reality in film is fictional or unreal – it is real but with a fictional apparatus. Interestingly, the recreation process can sometimes make a film's reality immortal; as soon as an image or a face is captured on film, it will no longer age. I am looking for a face that is chosen by the film to live in its reality and for me Hsiao-kang and Jean-Pierre both possess that special quality. Their faces were chosen by directors who make films in order to create art. When Truffaut chose Léaud from more than 1,000 boys who auditioned, and when I met Hsiao-kang in an arcade on the streets of Taipei, we both recognized that this is the face for the film reality we want to recreate. Actually, I think I take this approach even further than Truffaut. Whereas he used Léaud to recreate major events in the first half of his life, I just want to thoughtfully observe Hsiao-kang's face.

As Truffaut has his *Day for Night* (1973), so Tsai has *Goodbye, Dragon Inn* – both films made by men on the far side of forty reflecting on the medium to which they've given their lives, though the former is concerned with the circumstances of a film's production, the latter with those of exhibition and reception. The more aquatically inclined Taiwanese director imagines films not as – to borrow from Truffaut – trains passing in the night, but as monstrous frigates, unmoored and adrift, which carry their human cargo on a dark free-float.

Like his French predecessor, Tsai has a fascination with the peculiar alchemy of filmgoing, as can be seen in a striking moment that occurs about a third of the way into *Goodbye, Dragon Inn*, just after Chen opens a service door adjacent to the screen. Dwarfed by the projected images, she stops a moment to watch a scene in which actress Shangguan Lingfeng strides towards a waiting ambush, deftly side-stepping and slapping aside a sudden battery of enemy arrows that come whistling her way. From here, Chen steps back to a vantage behind the screen, and

Tsai cuts to a close-up of her raptly watching the film from cover of darkness, a meshwork pattern thrown across her face by the light of the projector as it penetrates the screen's porous surface. In a rapid-fire editing pattern that has no precedent in this slow-moving film and will be repeated at no point, Tsai cuts between Chen's upturned face and that of Shangguan, surveying her attackers with imperious disdain. In this cinema-set movie in which the action on the screen is often a mere backdrop for characters whose preoccupations are elsewhere, here is a moment of total engagement. The exact nature of the engagement, however, is ambiguous.

An interest in watching people in the process of watching people has always been crucial to Tsai's cinema, full as it is of muted longing from afar. Over time, this has come to include an increased emphasis on how people-watching from the shelter of spectatorship comprises one of the chief inducements of moviegoing. In *What Time Is It There?*, we see Hsiao-kang sitting alone in his room, lit only by the television's fluid light, watching the bootlegged copy of *The 400 Blows*, in mute dialogue with an image of Antoine Doinel, diminished but still very much intact behind a pane of Sony glass. The unadorned presentation of the scene, which unfolds within one of the staid, largely static frames that comprise the entire film, is deceptively simple. The contemplative pacing and Tsai's overarching richness of conception, however, help us to comprehend the preciousness of these two heartsick, never-to-meet young men unabashedly regarding one another across a darkened bedroom; of their two creators engaging in an impossible paternal-filial communion; of Lee's conjuring up his imagined love through images of a subtitled Paris; and of our own privilege watching and sharing in all of this in the dark. With only the sparest of means, we're located within an international, intergenerational, intertextual echo chamber of longing.

What, then, might Chen's character feel when looking up, wide-eyed, at Shangguan? It's an insoluble mystery – the mystery of what lies behind a human face in repose, which runs through so much of Tsai's work. Perhaps most notably, this includes the aptly titled *Face* and *Your Face*, the latter a 78-minute work comprised of thirteen static shots of thirteen subjects, some of them chatty, others mute. (A French analogue aside from Truffaut here suggests itself: the portraitist Philippe Garrel of 1974's *Les Hautes Solitudes*.)

We may, however, make certain inferences from what we know of the ticket seller. As in the case of Kiyonobu's Japanese tourist, as in the case of so many Tsai characters, Chen's character is defined in part by her thwarted desire – in this instance desire for her lone co-worker, to be inferred from her timorous approach to the projection booth, and from the gift she comes bearing, with evident discomfort.

Even more obviously, though, the character is defined by the source of that discomfort, her stumping hobble, which Tsai observes in a series of long shots in which she is seen painstakingly crossing the frame. (Tsai, as is evident in *Days*, is particularly interested in the ability of the moving image to document the body in compromise and breakdown.) If his development as a filmmaker up to the moment of *Goodbye, Dragon Inn* was distinguished by a gradual, if not entirely linear doing away with or wilful limitation of stylistic tools (travelling shots and camera movement in general, as well as non-diegetic music, which in *Goodbye, Dragon Inn* is limited to one piece at film's close) then this quality of slowness has since then only become increasingly central – in many cases to the point of near stasis. In recent years he has produced a series of *Walker* films, which feature Lee, in the garb of a Buddhist monk, making his way barefoot through a variety of urban spaces – Taipei, Hong Kong, Kuching, Marseilles, Tokyo – at an inchworm pace, moving like the minute hand on a clock.

The series was inspired by Tsai's fascination with the seventh-century scholar and monk Xuanzang, who embarked on a seventeen-year overland journey to India in order to study original Buddhist texts and correct misinterpretations that had slipped into them via translation. There are eight films in the *Walker* series so far; six shorts – *No Form, Walker, Sleepwalk, Diamond Sutra* (all 2012), *Walking on Water* (2013) and *No No Sleep* (2015) – and two feature-length: *Journey to the West* (2014) and *Sand* (2018). The conceptual approach of the films originated in the performance of Tsai's 2011 triptych theatrical piece, *Only You*, which featured a solo slow-walking scene by Lee – seventeen minutes in rehearsal, stretched to something like a half hour in the performance – the execution of which moved the director to pronounce: 'I have worked with you for twenty years and this is the moment I have been waiting for.'

To Lee's mind, his own innately unhurried biorhythms had long before begun to alter the pace of Tsai's work, seeping into the films themselves:

> Before he started to make feature films for the cinema, Tsai made a few TV series. I saw them for the first time in chronological order at a retrospective of his work in New York. It really struck me then how from *Vive L'Amour* onward the rhythm and speed of Tsai's style really changed. The rhythm gets much slower, the takes get longer, and there is less and less narrative. I think that this change, this slowing down has something to do with my influence. I remember the first time we worked together. The first two

> days went by without any problems but the third day was really hard. There was one simple movement, I had to turn my head and look at something. I had already done that four or five times and he said those shots were no good and had to be redone. He said, 'Lee Kang-sheng, can't you be a little more natural in this movement?' I remember we were on location and that day was really cold. I got angry because we did that shot so many times already, and I said, 'Well, this is how I naturally am.' I think that sentence was very important because up to that point he was probably working with the notion that there's some kind of standard motion for someone who turns his head. And also that there's a certain speed with which actors should talk. I did not have all these traditional notions of acting so I disrupted that way of thinking.

There is an echo here of French filmmaker duo Jean-Marie Straub and Danièle Huillet's annotation of their scripts, lining up every line reading to the breath of every performer, so that the performers' innate physical attributes – in this case, their lung power and natural tempo – determines the cadence at which the films move. For Tsai, this fascination with slowness, which reaches an apotheosis in the *Walker* series, is already very evident in the stump-stagger progress of Chen through the Fu-Ho Grand. What, though, might be the appeal of the fleet-footed wuxia to this most grounded of filmmakers, for whose characters flight in any sense is not an option?

The wuxia pian, as a genre, is defined in no small part by a defiance of gravity, a certain weightlessness – the ability of its dramatis personae to take to the air at will – accompanied as they do by the sound of flapping and fluttering silk garments, which, along with the liquescent clangour of swords, can be heard throughout *Goodbye, Dragon Inn*.

King Hu had, in fact, been present at the moment when the wuxia first developed its bouncing brio. Years before *Come Drink With Me* and *Dragon Inn*, he had played a role in Yue Feng's 1961 *The Swallow Thief*, an early Shaw Brothers martial arts effort starring Linda Lin-dai, which, though little remembered, has by some accounts an important role in the history of the genre. Years later, fight choreographer Han Yingjie would recall the watershed: 'I was the double for Linda Lin-dai and experimented with a seven by five foot trampoline. I did a somersault, the camera followed with a vertical pan, and the "weightless leap" was born.'

So began, per Han, the commonplace use of the trampoline technique, which allowed spring-heeled onscreen combatants to soar through the air with the greatest of ease. Further range of motion would be achieved through the development of wirework or wire fu, in which, by virtue of a cable and pulley system attached to a harness either hidden beneath an actor's costume or removed later through green screen, a performer may run up walls and land gracefully after multiple-storey leaps. (The technique was refined in Hong Kong but imported in time to Hollywood, with the Wachowskis' 1999 *The Matrix*, featuring fight choreography by Hong Kong legend Yuen Woo-ping and elements of gun fu à la John Woo, a key crossover text.)

It seems almost every high-profile Chinese filmmaker, even the most unlikely, has at one time or another the urge to make a wuxia – Wong has his *Ashes of Time* (1994) and *The Grandmaster* (2013); Hou has his *The Assassin* (2015), characteristically shot for muted obfuscation rather than snap and crackle; and Jia Zhangke's *A Touch of Sin* (2013), the English title of which alludes to Hu, draws inspiration from both the myth of the White Snake and the tragic migrants of *Water Margin*.

Goodbye, Dragon Inn is as near as Tsai has come to making the plunge, though he does stage musical numbers in both *The Hole* and *The Wayward Cloud*, and the proximity between the musical and the Chinese fight film has been much commented on – it was novelist Donald E. Westlake who observed 'Jackie Chan is Fred Astaire, and the world is Ginger Rogers' – both being defined by set pieces immortalising physical performances that stand outside the main narrative flow of the movie, both being capable of inspiring a rare sort of tingling elation in the viewer.

Writing on Hong Kong action cinema and the roots of the wuxia in the 'rhythmic theater' that is Peking opera, film theorist David Bordwell discusses the particular joy inspired by the best of these pop movies:

> Why do we leave these films not only tired but jubilant? Why do we think we can do anything? Partly because the kinetics have stamped the action's rhythm onto our senses; but also, I think, because the very cogency of the presentation has invited us to feel something of what supreme physical control might be like. ... In the best Hong Kong sequences, we rejoice in cinema's power over the physical world.

The quality can be found in the aerial combats of Hu's films, or in Astaire and Cyd Charisse's extended 'Girl Hunt' number in Vincente Minnelli's *The Band Wagon* (1953), or, for a young Graham Greene filing film criticism at *The Spectator*, in the 'lyrical absurdity' of Sacha Guitry's *Bonne Chance!* (1935). Such transports, for Greene, were something like the quintessence of cinema, a medium, like music, defined by its capacity to convey 'this sense of poignant happiness, the quickness and lightness and transience of a sensation you cannot call by any name so heavy as joy: "the phoenix hour": the nearest to a Utopia poor mankind is ever likely to get.'

And thank God we can get the sensation somewhere, but we need art and artists for our dark days, too – and quickness, lightness and joy are not the sensations in which Tsai traffics. If Shangguan's fighter in *Dragon Inn* represents a fantasy of supreme physical control, Chen's ticket taker in *Goodbye, Dragon Inn* recalls us to the ungainliness of fallible bodies made of skin, blood, and bone, and to the often onerous reality of having to be a person in the world. Like ourselves, then, it is reasonable to suppose that looking up at the screen, Chen has a glimpse of utopia, of a world without unending ache, in which staircases can be mounted in a single bound rather than a succession of excruciating steps.

The confrontation of Chen and Shangguan notwithstanding, Tsai cuts rarely and deliberately so that every edit feels like an event; Hu, like his contemporary Chang Cheh, cut more briskly than was the norm at the time, and inspired future

Hong Kong directors to do the same. It was these filmmakers in the seventies who, per Bordwell, began 'that era of breathlessly accelerated tempo – whirlwind action scenes, conversations ever on the move, rapidly changing angles, constantly mobile camera – that we associate with modern Hong Kong film.'

For de Villiers, the juxtaposition that occurs between Hu's 'breathless' cinema, projected on the Fu-Ho screen, and Tsai's contemplative cinema, the world of *Goodbye, Dragon Inn*, is at essence an encounter between the classical and the modern, between the movement-image and the time-image, as defined by Gilles Deleuze. *Goodbye, Dragon Inn*, however, obeys an emotional rather than a formal or rigidly conceptual logic. There is no real-time gimmickry, or indeed anything that might distract from a moment to moment attention to the characters, their movements, their quiet despairs. Though the "slower" film, Tsai's is shorter by a half hour than Hu's. While *Goodbye, Dragon Inn* gives the impression of occurring in real time, it actually telescopes the runtime of Hu's 111-minute film, which is only playing in the Fu-Ho for the first hour of *Goodbye, Dragon Inn*'s total 82 minutes.

For Tsai's own part, he has identified a deeper affinity, beyond surface differences, tying his own work to that of Hu:

> He's a literary as much as an action director, who was making his films during a very commercial period, which is why his wuxia films are so different from those of others. They're much more about real life. The rest have a much more romantic imagination – people flying around, riding horses – but King Hu's films have a much more realistic historical backdrop. There's a similarity between our films in that both of us are less interested in making films for escapism. We're both more interested in expression, even if it's an expression of genre.

The nature of the expression, of course, is very different. Hu's people take to the air while Tsai's are resoundingly, grudgingly, trudgingly down to earth. Cinema offers us transports, but those transports must finally end with the return to reality, and the closing of the velvet curtain on that sliver of utopia.

8.

It doesn't last long. As the final reel of *Dragon Inn* plays, Shih's eyes brim with tears – he is no longer the young and spry and invulnerable xia of Hu's film, but a frail, sentimental old man. (From Yang Kuei-mei's torrential weeping jag in Daan Forest Park at the end of *Vive L'Amour* to this moment to *Stray Dogs*, Tsai is with David Lynch the modern filmmaker whose scenes of crying most consistently carry genuine pathos.) From that familiar behind-the-curtain vantage, the ticket taker watches the film's closing image, a sun peering through a scrim of cloud coverage, setting over a body of water and casting its rays across the surface in a yellow-orange beam. In a wide shot facing the auditorium, the house lights flicker on to reveal a theatre already empty, as though the audience has evaporated without a trace, and for some five minutes we watch Chen going about her usherette duties, making her way up and down the aisles of the cinema, sweeping as she goes. This is followed immediately by the lobby meeting between Shih and Miao, and their pronounced moratorium:

> Miao: I haven't seen a movie in a long time.
>
> Shih: No one comes to the movies anymore. And no one remembers us anymore.

This is as near we come to an in-the-flesh connection, condolence or consummation onscreen. The Japanese tourist is brushed off from one near encounter with a blunt 'sayonara', and is last seen fleeing from a woman (Yang) who sidles up behind him, announcing her presence by cracking watermelon seeds with her teeth – it might be sexual panic that causes his retreat, it might be fear at the almost supernatural stealth with which she appears to a young man on guard for ghosts, or it might be some combination of the two. Chen observes a cat that has wandered in to take shelter from the rain, but doesn't move to pet it or shoo it away. Lee rewinds the print in the projectionist's booth, but time isn't turned back so easily, and the Fu-Ho's fate is sealed. Before leaving the theatre, he picks up the half bun left in the steamer, without a word of thanks or indeed a word. And Chen sets out on her last painful walk, into a rainstorm that has not slackened.

As Chen's character hobbles out into the deluge, there is a sudden swell of orchestral music on the soundtrack, and a woman's voice is heard, mournfully singing:

> I remember, under the moon
> I remember, before the flowers
> So much of the past lingers in my heart

The song, composed by Hattori Ryōichi and featuring lyrics by Chen Dea-yi, is 'Can't Let Go', performed by Yao Lee, one of the 'Seven Great Singing Stars' who dominated the Mandopop airwaves of Chinese popular culture of the thirties and forties, when the culture industry, as depicted in *Shanghai Blues*, was still largely based in Shanghai. The period is one of persistent fascination for Tsai, whose play *Only You*, revolving around a chanteuse-like character, takes its title from a song by Singing Star Li Xianglan – that is, Shirley Yamaguchi, the stealth Japanese leading diva of the Manchukuo Film Association.

Yao Lee, a Shanghai native, began performing on the radio in 1935 when she was thirteen, signed to the transnational behemoth Pathé Records two years later and, in 1949, fled at the height of her fame to Hong Kong. 'It was a very famous song,' Tsai has said of her 'Can't Let Go':

> Everyone from this generation can hum the tune ... Yao Lee dominated the thirties and forties in Shanghai and the fifties and sixties in Hong Kong. At that time, she was the pop singer sensation. She made many records. Her voice also appeared in many films and people used to say she had the voice of an angel. When she uses a deep, sorrowful voice to sing the blues, even listening to it now, it sounds very modern.
>
> When we mention Yao Lee, we also have to mention her famous songwriter brother, Yao Ming. Yao Lee used to sing with a very high voice and soft tone. In the forties, foreign movies started becoming very popular in Shanghai. Yao Ming listened to the singing of Black people

> in those movies and started writing songs of that flavour for Yao Lee. She was to sing lower, rougher, and with a taste of the West. Later on, Yao Lee started to take a liking to Patti Page, seeing Patti Page as her idol and imitating her ways of singing and her emotions. Yao Ming was a giant among popular songwriters, writing thousands of songs. After he passed away, Yao Lee would not listen to the radio for three years because her brother's songs were always playing.

The appeal of this story – the faded Singing Star, unsettled by the memory of her late brother, unable to listen to the radio – to one of Tsai's saturnine disposition should be obvious. It is worth noting here that *Bú sàn*, the Mandarin title of Tsai's film, translates as 'No Leaving'. Can't let go, can't let go...

In 2019, at the Venice premiere of a new restoration of *Goodbye, Dragon Inn*, Tsai took the stage to perform his own rendition of 'Can't Let Go'. He has in life a record of warbling in public, but in his work is choosy about when and where to deploy a song. Original non-diegetic music disappeared from Tsai's movies after his first two features; *Rebels of the Neon God* came, at the behest of CMPC's Xu, with an earworm synth theme courtesy of composer Huang Shu-jun, and *Vive L'Amour* has a short closing theme.[1] In later films, however, his affinity for 'oldies' asserts itself.

Tsai's fourth feature, *The Hole* – set in a dank and almost totally evacuated Taipei, and focusing on the rather drab routines of its two characters – contains his first musical numbers. These are threadbare-glamorous set pieces, which in their lip-synched delivery of familiar Mando-pop tunes recall the 'musical trilogy' of UK television serials written by Dennis Potter (1978's *Pennies From Heaven*, 1986's *The Singing Detective*, 1993's *Lipstick on Your Collar*) – or the short-lived American series *Cop Rock* (1990). Potter's trilogy utilise the popular songs of the Anglo-American airwaves in, respectively, the thirties, forties and fifties; the characters suddenly break mid-scene from their ostensible reality to mouth the words of vintage recordings. The Brechtian device, of Potter's invention, does away with the unacknowledged imposture of the classical musical number, emphasising the essential artifice of the trope of spontaneously bursting into song while providing a vantage on the pop radio-furnished interior lives of his characters.

For Potter, who very likely would have been acquainted with the pessimistic prognostications on popular culture in the capitalist world by the Frankfurt School or F.R. Leavis, there's something suspect about the tunes that are used to broadcast internalised fantasies in his serial works – a bit of treacle to make the brimstone of modern life go down, an opiate for the masses, imagined to be not much more self-aware than the anaesthetised yobs sleepwalking their way through the Margate fun-fair in Lindsay Anderson's *O Dreamland* (1953). As Potter has it: 'Cheap songs so called actually have something of the Psalms of David in them. They do say the world is something other than it is.'

While Tsai acknowledges the gulf that exists between pop's promises and life's hard facts, his affection for the 'cheap songs' of his youth, and the vision of another world that they offer, is undiminished by this understanding. Potter gives us characters afflicted and imprisoned by the impossible expectations fostered within their bosoms by Tin Pan Alley and Denmark Street, while there's a sense that Tsai regards himself as one of the fellow afflicted, and one who also hopes to be healed by the ministrations of pop's minstrels.

The eruptions of song in *The Hole* seem to exist in a parallel universe: sometimes accompanied by backup singers and dancers, they are mouthed by actress Yang Kuei-mei, who also plays the film's downstairs neighbour, though there is no clear linkage between Yang the neighbour and Yang the sultry singer. Tsai is not above an ironic counterpoint – a cut from a sneezing Yang, beset by symptoms of the mystery fever that has emptied the city, leads to her performance of a song called 'Achoo Cha Cha' in a pink sequined dress, being swooned over by four tuxedoed men – but, in contrast to Potter's use of such sequences to reveal his characters' secret hearts, the fantasy reveries seem rather to belong to Tsai himself.

His musical numbers 'are weapons that I use to confront the environment,' Tsai said at the close of the millennium. 'Because I think that toward the end of the century a lot of qualities – such as passionate desire, naive simplicity – have been suppressed. The musicals contain those qualities. It's something that I use psychologically to confront that world.'

The songs in *The Hole* are courtesy of Grace Chang, or Ge Lan, the Hong Kong-based chanteuse who became a screen and radio superstar in the fifties and early sixties for the Cathay Organisation, Shaw's predecessor for local market dominance. (Her music also features in *The Wayward Cloud*.) In *The Hole* we are treated to 'Tiger Lady' and 'I Want Your Love' and 'I Don't Care Who You Are' and 'Oh, Calypso' – the last of which Chang herself can be seen performing in Evan Yang's 1959 *Air Hostess*, a shiny, colourful bauble from Cathay that's something like an advertisement for Jet Age cosmopolitan modernity and VIP commercial luxury. Here, it's dropped into a Christmas light-spangled elevator sitting in the cold lobby of an empty, nondescript apartment block – a splash of glamour in an environment otherwise utterly devoid of it.

Writing on *Only You*, critic Andrew Chan notes the debt that Tsai owes to 'the bygone era of pop culture that influenced him as a kid – one that he came into contact with as symbols of dreamy Chinese sophistication on the Malaysian airwaves.' Here, too, a parallel with Terence Davies is appropriate – but rather than the likes of Cole Porter, or Debbie Reynolds's 'Tammy', used in *The Long Day Closes*, Tsai looks back to a lost pop paradise soundtracked by Chang, Lee, Li and the other Singing Stars, including his father's favourite, Zhou Xuan.

Following the model of studio-era Hollywood, Hong Kong and Taiwan's entertainment industries have long placed a premium on synergy, cultivating triple-threat stars with movie, television and Mando- or Cantopop careers, and marketing movies with tie-in albums – much like the Reynolds song, which appeared in 1957's *Tammy and the Bachelor*, and topped the Billboard chart for five weeks. As Universal-International handled Reynolds in the West, so Cathay handled Chang in the East.

Putting ourselves in the place of a sensitive young aesthete with a taste for beauty growing up in Kuching in the early sixties, it's not difficult to imagine the appeal of these songs drifting out into the city's balmy nights, or of the films seen in the city's cinemas, films sometimes featuring the very same songs, the result of strategies that made possible these monocultural Gesamtkunstwerks. (Indeed, Tsai credits the Shaw Brothers films for introducing him to tracks like his favourite oldie, 'Lover's Tears', with lyrics again courtesy Chen Dea-yi.) To this we can add the intangible allure that 'dreamy Chinese sophistication' might pose to the child of still recently settled immigrants abroad – and the degree to which, in the politically divided Greater China, popular culture has served to provide a unifying sense of home in the absence of an agreed-upon representative regime.

This function is illustrated with enormous sensitivity and feeling in one of the last great films of pre-Handover Hong Kong, Peter Chan's 1996 *Comrades: Almost a Love Story,* which follows Mainlanders played by Maggie Cheung and Leon Lai from their arrival in Hong Kong to their immigration to New York City. Throughout their travels, they are followed by the music of Teresa Teng, the Taiwanese-born chanteuse who was a pan-Asian icon for nearly thirty years, beginning with a prize-winning performance in 1964 of a song from *The Love Eterne* and ending in 1995 with her premature death in Thailand. Of the peculiar ubiquity of Teng throughout the Chinese world, *New Yorker* critic Hua Hsu writes:

> There's [a] popular saying: Wherever there are Chinese people, there is Teresa Teng's music. I never appreciated her symbolism as a child, back when her music seemed soft and ubiquitous. But it's not hard to imagine how Teng's songs about love and distance spoke to the various migrations and political estrangements throughout the Chinese-speaking world. For immigrants throughout the Chinese diaspora, her music was a reminder of their journeys, an excuse to indulge in nostalgia, three or four minutes at a time.

Such an indulgence concludes *Goodbye, Dragon Inn*. 'Can't let go, can't let go / I'll remember with longing forever' – the plaint in Yao Lee's voice carries with it a yearning for a remembered past wholeness, a holistic unity seemingly now cut off forever. Like those of many successful pop songs, the lyrics are flexible enough to be suited to almost any listener's personal use while the delivery renders them as achingly personal. They speak to romantic disappointment, but to something more as well, for as Chen passes out of the frame, the shot lingers a while longer on the exterior of the Fu-Ho, as if to address Yao Lee's longing towards the old cinema itself.

Tsai was not alone among Chinese filmmakers in being pursued by the persistent, plaintive memory of the pop culture of his youth. Tsui Hark – like Tsai, a Chinese kid raised abroad – had grown up knowing his ancestral homeland through the movies he saw in Saigon cinemas; in 1992 he released *New Dragon Gate Inn*, his remake of King Hu's classic, and then returned to the source in 2011 with *Flying Swords of Dragon Gate*. In 2000, Ang Lee, old habitué of the Chuang Mei Theatre, had an international box office smash with *Crouching Tiger, Hidden Dragon* – a film that owes an enormous debt to Hu, particularly *A Touch of Zen*, from which Lee remade and adapted the famous high-flying bamboo forest fight. In the midst of a crisis period for Hong Kong and Taiwanese cinemas, Tsui and Lee's films sought to channel the spirit of the sixties wuxia – to make 'em like they used to, the way nobody does anymore. Tsai's film doesn't propose a full-bodied resurrection as possible, but rather describes the pop past as a phantom presence: *Do you know this theatre is haunted?*

The idea of the haunted city, and the persistence of a city's past in the present, possesses a number of films from Greater China at the turn of the millennium, particularly those being made in pre-Handover Hong Kong; Stanley Kwan's *Rouge* (1987), in which the ghost of a courtesan who suicided in thirties Hong Kong reappears in the unrecognisable contemporary city, is one archetypal example. For Ackbar Abbas, writing in his study *Hong Kong: Culture and the Politics of Disappearance*, the figure of the ghost is a means to discuss the particular complexities of Hong Kong's vaporous, ungraspable cultural space. What, then, might Tsai be up to summoning cinematic spirits in the peculiar space that is Taipei?

A reference to 'hauntology' may be useful here. The term was introduced by Jacques Derrida in his 1993 *Spectres of Marx*, used to describe the continuing, ghostly presence of Marx's ideas in a world supposedly freed forevermore by the forces of neoliberal capitalism – in which the promise of a jet-setting future extended by films like *Air Hostess* had supposedly been fulfilled – to explain the degree to which, even after 1989, Marx's spectre of communism continued to haunt both Europe and points beyond. In the mid-2000s, the phrase was adapted by writers Mark Fisher and Simon Reynolds to discuss a loose confederation of artists, mostly UK-based musicians on the Ghost Box label – pronounced by Reynolds as 'consummate scavengers [who] trawl through charity shops, street markets and jumble sales for delectable morsels of decaying culture-matter.'

The sound of hauntology, as limned out by Fisher and Reynolds, is a corrupted one, born of the very fallibility of analogue recording mediums, which grow old and acquire wear and tear, just as we humans do – the process recounted in Tsai and Lee's long collaboration. 'Unlike digital formats,' Reynolds writes, 'analogue degrades through overuse: each listener kills the sound she loves.' As he notes, the title of the seventh studio album by hauntology-adjacent American musician Ariel Pink – *Worn Copy*, issued the same year as *Goodbye, Dragon Inn* – is here relevant. Pink's sensibility is grounded in eighties Day-Glo pop, but the sound is ever so slightly off, bent, giving the impression of a tune half-heard and half-remembered, encountered drifting from a stranger's open window or bleeding through the wall of a neighbouring room. (The muffled, muted soundtrack of Hu's *Dragon Inn* in Tsai's film suggests a possible parallel.)

Just as each listener kills the sound she loves, the twentieth-century cinemagoer was the witness to a process of a slow dying. You never watch the same print twice, and a film reel's every passage through a projector adds a degree of attrition and patina, until you arrive at the mangled specimens so well evoked by the critic Manny Farber in his 'Underground Films': 'prints that seem overgrown with jungle moss, soundtracks infected with hiccups.' While Tsai doesn't incorporate the physical decay of the film element into *Goodbye, Dragon Inn* – as does, say, Bill Morrison in his 2002 *Decasia*, assembled from strips of nitrate film in varying states of disintegration – he does break up *Dragon Inn*, partitioning it into unsatisfying fragments, letting its voice be muted by the cinema walls, the teasing and ultimate disintegration of its narrative pleasures amounting to yet another failure of consummation.

Contrasting hauntological acts whose work incorporates and comments on history against retro-pop artists who produce reasonable simulacra of past styles, Reynolds distinguishes hauntology for its 'ache of longing – for history itself' in the face of an ahistorical pop present. That 'ache' figures into the definition of a word that has often been associated with Tsai. 'It's delicate, but potent... in Greek, nostalgia literally means the pain from an old wound. It's a twinge in your heart, far more powerful than memory alone' – this comes courtesy the fictional character Don Draper, played by Jon Hamm, delivered during a campaign for a Kodak Carousel slide projector in a 2007 episode of *Mad Men*, part of the wave of prestige television that we've been told again and again has dethroned cinema in the public imagination. The programme's success exemplified the phenomenon that is also its subject: the supremacy of ballyhoo in American life, or perhaps the life of the developed world as a whole.

Nostalgia can be heartstrings-tugging a sales pitch. It can be an inspiration, looking to the past from an unendurable present to find possible futures not taken. It can be an entirely regressive force, responsible for the present morass of American popular culture, in which proven IP are rehashed ad nauseam for an audience consigned to eternal adolescence, a landscape cluttered with over-familiar talismans like the virtual reality OASIS of Spielberg's *Ready Player One* (2018). In *Times Square Red, Times Square Blue*, Delany writes of nostalgia that it 'presupposes an uncritical confusion between the first, the best, and the youthful gaze (through which we view the first and the best) with which we create origins.'

The Greeks that Draper cites thought nostalgia a sickness, and certainly there is something more than a little morbid in the latter-day works of nostalgist par excellence Woody Allen, whose contemporary young people are little old men and women who venerate the popular culture of the Depression-era America into which Allen was born, and its bygone analogue textures – like Christina Ricci in *Anything Else* (2003) condemning the 'sterilised' sound of CDs, or Timothée Chalamet's hysterically monikered Gatsby Welles in *A Rainy Day in New York* (2019) announcing, 'I just like to watch old movies and play my vinyl.' Quentin Tarantino, a known *Anything Else* booster and Shaw Bros. superfan (who cribbed their logo for his 2003 vintage genre-movie bricolage piece *Kill Bill: Volume 1*), has clout enough to have established himself as a one-man bulwark against the rising digital tide – where Tsai has his modest Café Corridor, Tarantino has his 300-seat New Beverly Cinema revival house in Los Angeles, showing a bill of 35mm and 16mm double features, many from the filmmaker's own collection.

Though it seems today to anticipate the phenomenon of digital cinema, *Goodbye, Dragon Inn* cannot be counted as a response to it. Tsai's film never directly addresses the matter of format, which in Taipei in 2003 would have been no issue outside of competition from the MTV trade, the film vs. digital debate not having yet begun in earnest. For his part, Tsai seems to have no difficulty envisaging a cinema without acetate. *Stray Dogs*, his first digital feature, makes room for multiple long takes that go beyond the capacity of a 1,000-foot magazine, and he attributes its final nocturnal images to the ability of digital to shoot in low-light environs. In his ease with adopting new technology, he differs from such varied staunchly pro-film figures as celluloid supremacist Tarantino and digital sceptic Babette Mangolte, who sees a fundamental problem in the format's ability to mark duration – as Tsai's work, especially the *Walker* films, endeavour to do. She writes, 'Even if a film isn't creating an experiential sense of time, it can evoke it, but the digital film is at a disadvantage in this regard.' For Tarantino, quoted in 2012, the inferiority of digital presentation is axiomatic, because digital projection is nothing more than 'television in public'.

For Tsai, one suspects, the crucial part of that equation is the 'public' – the nostalgia for moviegoing as a shared experience, at a moment when it sometimes seems our viewing habits have in a little over a century gone full circle from the solitary experience of the nickelodeon Kinetoscope to the laptop or Oculus Rift. We all have our different ways of holding on, or of surrendering to the onrushing flow of time. *Crouching Tiger, Hidden Dragon* and *Goodbye, Dragon Inn*, for example, are both films made by ethnically Chinese men born in the mid-fifties and based at one time or another in Taiwan, but where Lee attempts to channel the spirit of Hu, even casting *Come Drink With Me*'s 'Golden Swallow' Cheng Pei-pei in a key role, Tsai ruefully acknowledges that you can't go home again. *Dragon Inn* has not changed, but the audience has. The transnational cultural community to which Tsai belonged in his youth, made up of residents of a China of the mind, still exists, but its centre has shifted again, from Hong Kong to Beijing, and many of its movies have metastatised into blockbusters made on the Hollywood scale, usually with even less charm.

But in *Goodbye, Dragon Inn* we encounter a present haunted by the pop past – not only that, but by a past envisioning of the past, exemplified by the double nostalgia of 'Can't Let Go', a longing for an antique expression of longing, reaching for a happier time. It is a farewell to cinema – or to one definition of cinema, as well as to generations of Greater Chinese popular culture now fallen out of reach, to the Shaw Brothers and the Seven Great Singing Stars. It tributes the communities whose dreams were furnished and decorated by these bright, melancholy pop products, and the temples in which they convened, the movie houses that were expiring en masse as the millennium turned. And in making this tender parting gesture, Tsai poses a pretty dilemma to himself and to cinema at large: where do you go after you've said goodbye?

1 *The Skywalk Is Gone*, like *Goodbye, Dragon Inn*, has no song-and-dance numbers, but a closing tune, 'Nanping Bell', one of the bright-eyed, innocent minded *xiaoyuan mingge* (campus folk songs) that were turned out of Taiwan in great number in the mid-seventies, and which in turn greatly influenced the popular *xinyao* (Singapore ballads) of the eighties.

9.

If *Goodbye, Dragon Inn* were only a maudlin nostalgia piece bemoaning the passing of a lost, better time, it would be of limited interest, but Tsai's ironic humour, self-awareness and intelligence make it something far richer. Speaking to the eulogistic quality of his film, he is circumspect about what is being mourned. 'Oldies are the background music of my youth,' he said while promoting the film in 2004:

> After growing up, I still like to listen to them. I often find many emotions in these old songs. Is this reminiscence? I don't know... I just know that no one has the power to bring back the past; not an era or your own youth. Nor even can someone stop a theatre from being torn down.

> The world moves quickly. Now, people are satisfied watching DVDs at home or surfing the virtual world of the internet. But do you remember the late night showings in a theatre, where a thousand people would sit together, laugh together, cry together. Even the lightest sigh would move the heart.

This is the world evoked in *Goodbye, Dragon Inn*'s prologue – the world of the neighbourhood cinema, of popular art that was both popular and art, of an audience from all different backgrounds coming together to laugh and cry together. The film itself offers little in the way of hope that this world may be regained. 'From my point of view,' said Tsai, 'cinema's departure from the movie theater is part of a natural progression of things.'

Here it may be useful to remember the crucial role of Buddhism in Tsai's filmography, which well predates the *Walker* series. The title of *Rebels of the Neon God* refers, in part at least, to the deity Nezha, whom Hsiao-kang's mother becomes convinced her son is the reincarnation of. In *The River*, Hsiao-kang is subjected to a litany of Buddhist healing rituals. In *What Time Is*

It There?, the death of his father is followed by Buddhist mourning ceremonies, and afterwards his mother comes to believe that her recently deceased husband's soul has very likely returned to the family house – perhaps as a cockroach, perhaps as a large fish in the living room aquarium. In the film's conclusion, the image of a Ferris wheel reflected in the pool of the Tuileries Garden suggests the wheel of reincarnation, and immediately precedes the reappearance of the dead father in Paris – a wandering soul, a dream, or a rebirth?

Tsai's work allows us to draw our own conclusions as to where his spiritual leanings incline (see also his 2001 half-hour *A Conversation With God* in which, en route to record a famous medium, Tsai and Lee Kang-sheng, stuck in traffic, instead turn the camera on a roadside temple celebrating the birthday of a god). In understanding the nature of the 'goodbye' in *Goodbye, Dragon Inn*, we might consider the Buddhist concept of impermanence. The doctrine of impermanence, *anicca* in the Pali canon, is essential in the Buddhist cosmology, understood as one of the three marks of existence, along with *dukkha* (suffering) and *anattā* (non-self). As human experience is marked by cycles of birth, life, and death, so too are all things susceptible to the same pattern of creation and dissolution. As painful as it may be to contemplate, there is nothing unusual in the fact that cinema as experienced or understood in Tsai's youth – or in my youth, or in yours – should pass from the earth. Just as there is nothing remarkable in the prospect of it, having passed, then returning.

There is, perhaps, a long-view philosophical comfort in this notion of an undying and eternal essence, but we mere mortals still must contend with the practicalities pertaining to living and working in cinema at a time where the art form is both dying and being reborn with agonising labour pains. Reincarnation can be a bumpy ride.

Even before the film's Paris finale, the image of the wheel is seen many times in *What Time Is It There?*, and not always turning smoothly. When Hsiao-kang sits before *The 400 Blows*, he's watching the scene in which the young Doinel boards a carnival ride consisting of a round, recessed area walled in by what appears to be corrugated metal, placed in a tent that makes space for spectators above. When the ride begins, the "room" begins to spin on a central pivot point, pressing the riders – whose number includes a cameo-ing Truffaut – against the wall through centrifugal force, inspiring as it does a combination of giddiness and nausea. (Truffaut, too, was drawn towards the image of the wheel of life, like the tempestuously turning 'Le Tourbillon', the whirlwind of love that Jeanne Moreau sings of in 1962's *Jules and Jim*: 'We met each other, we met each other again / We lost sight of each other, over and over again.') The French version of this carnival ride circa the late fifties is called the Rotor. Some thirty years later in Cincinnati, I'd routinely ride something called the Gravitron that was in all essential points unchanged. In fairgrounds, at least, there seems to be some constancy in this world. As we have had occasion to note, the same cannot be said of the cinema, which, per some observers, has moved closer in recent years to its fairground origins, to a Cinema of Attractions.

These myriad changes have long been a point of preoccupation for Tsai, who, as well as any living director, has expressed the existential quandary that faces filmmakers treating cinema as an "art" medium when the institution of the arthouse is in danger: 'If box-office numbers had any correlation to the intrinsic value of one's film, every last filmmaker in the world would give great credence to those numbers,' Tsai told me in a 2015 interview. 'However, as my films have zero financial potential in this economy, the question for me becomes, how can I prove the value of my films? Why do I continue to make films? Who am I making them for?'

If, at the beginning of the century, *What Time Is It There?* and *Goodbye, Dragon Inn* seemed to signify Tsai taking a place of privilege in what we might call contemporary cinema or the international arthouse, they retrospectively represent a high water mark of his visibility, to use an apt metaphor for Tsai, to be followed by a slow recession, a draining, a withdrawal.

Tsai's next film, *The Wayward Cloud*, returns to check in on Lee and Chen's characters from *What Time Is It There?* and *The Skywalk Is Gone.*

In one point of convergence with *Goodbye, Dragon Inn*, *The Wayward Cloud* had at one time been imagined as a grandmother-grandson story, with the old woman discovering her grandchild acting in adult films, but the idea was reconfigured when Ann Hui was unavailable to play the role of the grandmother.

The Wayward Cloud did surprisingly robust box office in Taiwan but, with its discomfiting sex scenes and gonzo musical numbers – including one in which women dressed as flowers writhe around a statue of former President Chiang Kai-shek – it didn't fit the established pattern of Tsai's career progression to date, which could be conveniently narrativised as a journey towards an ever-increasing austerity, and tied in with a "slow cinema" movement – this being a buzzy phrase that had begun to gain traction at the time. (Woe betide the auteur who fails to stick to the script that the critical commentariat has written for them; witness the befuddled reaction to countryman Hou's uncharacteristically adrenalised *Millennium Mambo* in 2001.) *The Wayward Cloud* had only a few surfacings stateside, these briefly glimpsed, before scudding off out of sight.

Tsai had continued producing films at a steady clip after *Rebels of the Neon God*, but the four-year wait for a new theatrically released feature between *Face* and *Stray Dogs* was the longest in his career, only to be outdone by that which followed. *Stray Dogs* is Tsai's tenth and last feature to date to have a commercial run in the US. Until recently, with the announcement of *Days*'s intended US theatrical release in 2021, there was reason to believe it may be the final, as Tsai spoke quite freely of his exhaustion with the hustle involved in traditional feature filmmaking. He is not alone in his fatigue. Even brand-name American auteurs like Lynch and John Waters have concluded that the process of getting a film made under the right circumstances, never easy in the best of times, has become too gruelling to contemplate.

Stray Dogs finds Lee, the skinny kid from *Rebels of the Neon God*, having now taken on both the physical and existential weight of middle age. He is working as a human billboard advertising real estate – the same boom and bust industry at the centre of *Vive L'Amour* – paid a pittance to plant himself on a median in a busy intersection. Tsai's inspiration, once again, comes from direct experience and observation of the urban environment, a sighting of a man fulfilling that demeaning job on the streets of Taipei. Those inclined to seeking cinephiliac references may also detect an echo of another, much older film concerned with urban isolation and the experience of being subsumed in an audience, King Vidor's *The Crowd* (1928), though more pertinent perhaps is the Hou-directed episode that lends its title to the omnibus movie that it leads off, 1983's *The Sandwich Man* – one of the key films of the nascent Taiwanese New Wave.

For many, these New Wave films constitute a Golden Age. Tsai has also used the term to describe the years of his own early moviegoing, the years that produced *Dragon Inn*, for in the very idea of a Golden Age there is an inference of stability, of a long and peaceful reign – a senescent prosperity enjoyed under a wise ruler, rather than the tyranny of malevolent eunuchs which opens Hu's film, or the digital upheaval that had already begun to radically reshape the industry in 2003. When the phrase is used with regards to cinema, it often indicates, for example, the at least sporadically benevolent dictatorship of the Hollywood studios, or of Mexico City studios of the *Época de Oro*, or the market dominance of the Shaw Brothers, who kept the product turning out thanks to a vertically integrated international production and distribution system that serviced cinemas from Singapore to Kuching.

Hu had in fact turned his back on that stability, rejecting both the predictable pains and the security of being a Shaw Brothers contract director to pursue what Tsai called a 'lonely and difficult road of filmmaking'. He fled the luxuriously appointed Movietown plantation in order to work on his own terms, or something closer to them, in a new country with a fraction of the resources. And he thrived – or at least for a time. Hu was a legendary perfectionist: he provided the classical calligraphy for his opening credits himself; laboured over his soundtracks and the choreography of music and image, as almost no wuxia director did; and would spend fully twenty-five days on the bamboo forest scene in his *A Touch of Zen* to get it just so. Though this tendency to nitpick didn't hamper Hu's career so long as he delivered solid hits, it sank him when he moved away from martial arts spectacle to produce a pair of 1979 films shot in South Korea and deeply invested in Buddhist hermeneutics, *Raining in the Mountain* and *Legend of the Mountain*.

Tsai's other known art hero, Truffaut, hacked out his own lonely and difficult trail, setting up his production company, Les Films du Carrosse, and operating as one of the few conspicuous independent successes in an increasingly studio-backed or state-funded French film industry. In some respects, the road of the stubbornly individualist filmmaker, like Hu, like Truffaut, like Tsai – who runs his own production company with Lee, Homegreen Films, and, with the exceptions of *Rebels of the Neon God* and *Goodbye, Dragon Inn*, has co-financed through French institutions – has never been more lonely and difficult. In 2006, Gore Vidal wrote that 'to speak today of a famous novelist is like speaking of a famous cabinetmaker or speedboat designer. Adjective is inappropriate to noun. How can a novelist be famous – no matter how well known he may be personally to the press? – if the novel itself is of little consequence to the civilized, much less to the generality?'

The reality of the famous filmmaker, too, has been called into question. The marginalisation of the novel as described by Vidal is not, necessarily, a death knell to the form – written paragraphs can be composed and distributed, on some level at least, with very slender means. The marginalisation of cinema, as described by Jones, offers a somewhat more complicated problem, for movies require cash on the barrelhead and, traditionally, filmmakers have been required to cultivate a certain level of public profile or critical cache in order to acquire that capital and bring the full resources of the industrial moviemaking apparatus to bear on their craft. When filmmakers get smaller, the pictures do too – or at least those shaped by individual rather than committee decisions. (That a wilfully minor-key, lo-fi artist like the South Korean Hong Sang-soo is today pointed to as a leading light of festival filmmaking is significant – we are a long ways from the ambitious undertakings of an Antonioni, a Truffaut, or even Yang and Tsai.)

In the sphere of pop cinema, the twenty-first century has witnessed a concerted effort to roll back the pre-eminent position established for the director-creator through decades of hard polemical street fighting, shifting consumer loyalty instead to intellectual property, which has the distinct advantage of lacking free will or the ability to talk back to management. There are certainly name-above-the-title auteurs who have emerged in the last two decades – Christopher Nolan being perhaps the most prominent such figure – but these are exceptions to prove the rule. Tsai, of course, never evinced the temperament or ambition to operate at the big-budget level, and the trajectory of his first fifteen years as a filmmaker follows what was a rather familiar plot for the postwar "art" director: a breakthrough debut, the gradual accrual of a body of work that refines the style, the arrival of the Mature Masterpieces. Roughly contemporary to Tsai's rise one can observe other filmmakers proceeding along approximately the same track – say, Claire Denis and

Wong as they progress from *Chocolat* and *As Tears Go By* (both 1988) to *Beau Travail* (1999) and *In the Mood for Love* (2000).

Today, in the commercial arthouse world, prospects are only marginally better for idiosyncratic and aesthetically ambitious filmmakers. The techno-utopian line has it that thanks to the ubiquity of affordable, lightweight, high resolution digital cameras it is easier than ever before to Just Make Your Film, and this is, for good and ill, true enough. There is still, however, the small problem of getting the thing in front of an audience – preferably a paying one – once it's been made. Said Tsai, 'I can't just be "a lone flower admiring itself". I want to be seen. That's why I create constantly. The goal is to increase the likelihood of being seen.'

Constant creation has not been Tsai's only tactic. He has, toward the end of getting himself before the public eye, extensively explored alternate distribution strategies, well before the need for such guerrilla tactics was yet evident. In 2000, Bruno Pésery, the French producer of *What Time*

Is It There?, sold Tsai the international copyright to the film for one euro. Given the opportunity to self-distribute in Taiwan by this windfall, he handled his show like a travelling Chautauqua assembly or a commedia dell'arte troupe... or the yellow cows of *All Corners of the World*:

> At that time, my films already had a bad reputation in Taiwan's theatrical circuit, and no one wanted to release them. I convinced a small hundred-seat [stage] theatre to rent their space to me for two weeks for my own theatrical run. A week before opening day, I took my actors to the streets to sell tickets to the film – for some strange reason, although no one in Taiwan came to see my films, my bald head was highly recognizable to local strangers – and after the first morning, astonishingly we had sold over 300 tickets. I quickly discovered a secret: in a regular theatrical release, my film would inevitably be up against about ten different commercial releases each week, and wouldn't even be given one-tenth of a fighting chance against those films, whereas if I sold tickets directly to a smiling stranger on the street, the chances

> of a positive outcome was 50/50, because the answer can only be *yes* or *no*. So I spent ten years selling tickets to my films – all starring Lee Kang-sheng – like this. The box-office numbers weren't miraculous, but they were also not disastrous. Sadly, there was no way to keep a proper record.

It was in the immediate aftermath of the release of *Goodbye, Dragon Inn*, as Tsai tells it, that still another strategy suggested itself. After seeing this work, which might be received as an SOS from a failing cinema, 'Many people from the art world began to get in touch with me,' he recalled. The year after the film's release, Cai Guo-Qiang, a New York-based Chinese contemporary artist, invited Tsai to participate in an exhibition at the Bunker Museum of Contemporary Art, held at a former army base-turned-museum on Kinmen Island in the Taiwan Strait – one of the primary lines of defence during the KMT retreat, routinely shelled for decades, and under military rule until 1992.

Tsai's contribution was *Withering Flower* (the fate of a lone flower, perhaps?). The piece was an installation set in a disused bunker, illuminated with candles and occupied by a massive bronze statue of Chiang Kai-shek turned to regard the shores of China, while the embrasures, empty of artillery, were filled with gauze – symbolic, per Tsai, of 'castration'. In a side room formerly used for munitions, a single-channel video showed clips from *The River* and filmed excerpts from a play by the Shanghai-raised novelist Eileen Chang, whose story, about a woman abandoned by a succession of choosy suitors, gives the piece its name. As in a shrine, visitors were invited to leave notes describing their hopes for the future.

More immediately pertinent to *Goodbye, Dragon Inn* is Tsai's piece *It's a Dream*, which began as part of a collection of three-minute shorts included in the anthology *To Each His Own Cinema*, commissioned in 2007 for the 60th anniversary of the Cannes Film Festival. To shoot the film, Tsai returned to his birth country. 'I went back to a cinema in Malaysia that I was very familiar with,' he said. 'This type of cinema was built in the 1950s, 1960s or even 1970s. ... Movie houses at that time weren't attached to a mall. They usually stood alone like temples. In those days people were dependent on movies: it was like a ritual for them.'

In its original form, the ritual-rich *It's a Dream* might be described as a memory film, as *The Glass Menagerie* is a memory play, though a surreal warping of the memories at hand is evident straightaways. Tsai, in voiceover, describes a dream in which he is eating durian with his father, who is still a young man, and his mother, 'already an old lady' (Lee Kang-sheng and Chay Yiok-khuan, Tsai's actual mother). The scene is depicted with the narrator as a small child, crouched by a lamp on the floor of a dark cinema – the imagining of a decimated family unit reunited.

The familiar figure of a movie-loving maternal grandmother then appears, seen in a black-and-white photograph propped against a cinema chair. 'Every time she took me to a movie,' the narrator says of the grandmother, 'she'd buy me pears on a skewer'. This introduces a scene of a woman (Pearlly Chua) alone at the cinema eating the described snack, pausing to offer it, without turning around, to a male spectator (Norman Bin Atun) seated behind her – an image that suggests both neighbourly conviviality and perhaps erotic invitation. Finally, the family – young father, smoking; old mother, silent; grandmother, only a photograph; and child – are seen sitting together, facing the screen as an oldie plays, 'Shi Meng Shi Zhen' by the then-recently deceased Gong Qiuxia, another of the Seven Great Singing Stars.

Imagined originally as something rather more sinister – according to Tsai, 'a film about a run-down cinema and about bad guys who entrap little children in the cinema and later traffic them to other countries' – *It's a Dream* emerged finally as a sort of postscript to *Goodbye, Dragon Inn*. And it, too, recalls the particular culinary tang of Alan Lau's paean to Kuching's old cinemagoing, with its memories of hot kacang, peanuts and melon seeds, just like those being cracked by Yang Kuei mei in *Goodbye, Dragon Inn*. (Compared to such concessions, the dusty desolation of multiplex popcorn seems especially depressing.)

It's a Dream would eventually be reconceptualised as a 23-minute installation – most of the runtime a long fade-out that gradually disappears each spectator, leaving only the grandmother's picture – which premiered the same year at the Venice Biennale, and was added to the permanent collection of the Taipei Fine Arts Museum. For the Biennale version, part of the Taiwanese pavilion called 'Atopia', Tsai recreated a miniature cinema using seats from the rural theatre where the film was shot. The social, people-watching element of moviegoing, as described in various terms by Barthes and Delany, as epitomised by the proffered pear slice in Tsai's movie, would be emphasised by the arrangement of the seats, which offered a vantage on not only the screen but also one's neighbours. Explaining the installation, Tsai said, 'You can feel that these chairs are the remains of the cinema. And when you are sitting in these chairs watching the film, you are actually watching a space that no longer exists.'

Tsai's feature filmmaking activity, too, has been increasingly impacted by his relationship with the art world, in Asia as well as in Europe. *I Don't Want to Sleep Alone*, released in 2006, was commissioned with Austrian money, for the 250th anniversary of the birth of Mozart. Three years later, his *Face* was shot inside, and underwritten in part by, the Musée du Louvre at the invitation of director Henri Loyrette (the first and to my knowledge only film produced for a proposed 'The Louvre Invites Filmmakers' collection). The completed film would premiere at the National Theatre in Taiwan, and Tsai described to me an encounter between a cultural department attaché and Loyrette:

> Someone asked him, 'Why did you choose to commission Tsai to make a film for the Louvre? Here, we can never understand what his films are about.' The reply was cryptic but brilliant: 'A lot of people can't understand Picasso's paintings, but it's this mystery that beckons for closer examination and study.' I thought about this and wondered: one could go to the gallery to study a mysterious Picasso, but where would one go to study a mysterious film? Is the answer the theater, where the limited spectrum of offerings usually only represent Hollywood? My films are made with an artistic intent, so why not show

> them in a gallery context? Can't one study cinema in the gallery as well?

This idea – that of the gallery as a space where the cinema can go to be reborn – recurs through Tsai's interviews in the years following his first forays into the white box. Of a Dutch curator's critique of *It's a Dream*, Tsai noted, 'He wrote ... that this movie announced the death of film and its resurrection. I totally agree with him. And he actually touched upon the key point of how I think about movies. It sounds like a contradiction, but movies need to leave today's theaters in order to be resurrected.' Or, if you prefer, reincarnated.

10.

There is a rich history of moving image-based work designed to be seen outside the parameters of traditional theatrical exhibition, parameters that weren't codified until some years on in the life of the medium. No one who watched Winsor McCay live on the vaudeville stage interacting with his animated *Gertie the Dinosaur* (1914), which seemed to obey his commands on cue, would have said they were watching a multimedia performance, though today we would call it exactly that. And no sooner had the single-screen, black box theatre been established as the standard for cinematic exhibition than artists began to tinker with it, to push at its parameters – see Oskar Fischinger's three-screen *Raumlichtkunst* (1926), or Abel Gance's use of Polyvision widescreen, a process involving the simultaneous projection of three reels in a horizontal row, to expand the frame of his *Napoleon* (1927).

Cinema's new cultural dominance exerted an influence on theatrical stagecraft, as well: Walter Gropius's Total Theater, designed for the German director Erwin Piscator in 1927 but ultimately unbuilt, included 'a system of spotlights and film projectors, transforming walls and ceiling into moving picture scenes'; Orson Welles's *Too Much Johnson* (1938) was made for integration into his Mercury Theatre troupe's production of William Gillette's play of the same name, though went unused; and Williams's early stage instructions for *The Glass Menagerie* even suggested the incorporation of slide projections.

Ongoing experiments in intermedia hybridisation, particularly those adjoining the gallery and cinema worlds, were crucial to the experimental film scene of the late fifties and sixties. The term 'expanded cinema' is attached to Gene Youngblood's proselytising 1970 book of the same name, but had been used to cover a whole host of artworks produced over the decade before that text appeared, as typified by those on view at the Expanded Cinema Festival, sometimes called the New Cinema Festival, put on by the Film-Makers' Cinematheque in November of 1965. Attractions included Stan VanDerBeek's *Movie-Mural*, an assemblage accomplished through the simultaneous operation of a dozen projectors, and Claes Oldenburg's *Moveyhouse*, in which an audience at the Film-Makers' Co-op theatre in the basement of the Wurlitzer Building was crowded into the side aisles to watch eight performers play out the roles of spectators and ushers while the screen was, at times, illuminated by a flashlight beam showing through the revolving blades of a fan.

Per scholar Andrew V. Uroskie, the mission of the expanded cinema

> might be understood as precipitating an analogous change of venue for the motion picture experience. It was comparatively easy to make different kinds of films, but much more difficult to change the way in which films were seen. ... However much they wanted to divorce themselves from Hollywood's model of industrial

> practice, its half-century dominion had established protocols for exhibition and spectatorship that had long since been internalized by layperson and connoisseur alike. … These artists discovered the need to grapple not simply with the forms of commercial cinema, but with these accepted norms of cinematic exhibition and spectatorship. The expanded cinema recognized that it was no longer sufficient to change the form of cinema: one needed to change the total situation within which the moving image was exhibited and seen as well as the context within which it was understood.

This mission is quite near to Tsai's own, and places his work in a long lineage of expanded cinema practice that runs on through to the landscape of unspooled 16mm film that accompanies the presentation of Jud Yalkut's *Destruct Film* (1967), the projected sculpture of *Line Describing a Cone* (1973) and Anthony McCall's other solid light works, or the mock cinema installation, titled *The Paradise Institute*, designed by Janet Cardiff and George Bures Miller for the Canadian Pavilion at the Venice Biennale in 2001 – the same year the Whitney mounted *Into the Light: The Projected Image in American Art 1964–77*, exploring the abundant intersections 'between the black box and the white cube' during this period. (Alongside these highbrow examples we might mention more widely accessible experiments in novelty haptics such as Smell-O-Vision's debut in the 1960 *Scent of Mystery* and William Castle's chair-buzzing Percepto!, which menaced audiences watching 1959's *The Tingler*.)

Tsai isn't by a long shot the first cineaste to carve himself a space in the gallery world, but the migration of a figure of his importance to a practice that's ever more reliant on gallery representation – during the years in life that often represent those of peak power for a director – does suggest a larger shift in film culture, something with implications that go beyond just Tsai's career. In increasing numbers, filmmakers have been finding a refuge, and an ancillary income stream, in the white box. Lynch, a trained sculptor and painter, and Waters, an art world gadfly, may have backed off from theatrical filmmaking, but both have had numerous showings of their plastic arts output since last having a wide theatrical release.

For those who don't produce *objets d'art* per se, the single- or multi-channel installation has been an in. Beginning in 1995 with *D'Est: au bord de la fiction*, a piece for twenty-five monitors commissioned by the Walker Art Center in Minneapolis, Chantal Akerman produced a series of works conceived (or re-conceived from material shot for film works) for the gallery – the last of these being the multi-channel *NOW* (2015), which premiered at the Venice Biennale. The roll call of established cineastes who've crossed into the art world is impressive and ever-expanding, including Agnès Varda, Harun Farocki, Werner Herzog, Pedro Costa, Abbas Kiarostami and Victor Erice. Others – like Lynn Hershman Leeson, Steve McQueen, Omer Fast and Sam Taylor-Johnson – made the leap to feature filmmaking, either permanently or temporarily, after first "emerging" in the white box context.

A concurrent gallery practice is maintained by many filmmakers whose breakthrough works appeared approximately contemporary to *Goodbye, Dragon Inn*, even in instances when they have no evident affinity for the space – Laura Poitras's 2016 show at the Whitney, *Astro Noise*, being one notable boondoggle. Other creators are more naturally amphibious, like Albert Serra, whose five-channel *Singularity*, commissioned for the Catalan Pavilion at the 2015 Venice Biennale, is for my money his most satisfying work, or Apichatpong Weerasethakul – in terms of critical and festival approbation, a shortlist shoo-in for the most important international filmmaker of the young century – who in a multi-screen work like the dreamy *Primitive* (2009), viewed by spectators recumbent on plush carpeting, finds a form perfectly suited to the loafing biorhythms of his art. Many younger filmmakers are even more nonchalantly exploring alternate exhibition spaces, as in the case of the current American crop, among them James N. Kienitz Wilkins, who has made work for gallery (2017's *The Republic*) and full-dome planetarium (2018's *The Dynamic Range*), or Zia Anger, whose *My First Film* (2019) is a live performance piece commentary on her abortive feature debut, toured through a variety of venues, both IRL and online.

Independent Chinese filmmakers subject to censorship at home and dependent on foreign viewership for their livelihood have found an important outlet in the gallery, like Zhao Liang, who has been making installations since starting out in the nineties, or Wang Bing, whose 14-hour *Crude Oil* was premiered as a single-channel projection at the 2008 International Film Festival Rotterdam, who'd commissioned the piece. (The festival, who also underwrote Apichatpong's *Sleepcinemahotel* installation/guest house dormitory in 2018, has been unusually responsive to such expanded cinema-type works.)

In Tsai's case, it appears that he views his gallery work both as of a piece with his filmmaking practice and, as he stated in reference to *Walker*, 'a conscious act of rebellion against the way cinema is perceived in today's society.' In a conference at the National Central University in Taiwan in 2010, Tsai further articulated the nature of his rebellion:

> Life is business, life is competition. We see how the directors squeeze themselves only to produce box-office success. We see how the

> politicians intend to persuade people that economic development should come first, regardless of the fact that the ozone layer is getting thinner and thinner as global warming becomes more and more serious, and that the earth cannot withstand more exploitation. In this weakened environment, an era of recycling is coming. I think everything should be stopped, including my lecture here, my movie production, everything.

In 21st-century political and aesthetic discourse, the phrase 'accelerationism' is increasingly prevalent, succinctly describable as a full-steam-ahead philosophy that now often comes hand in hand with a conviction that the existing order of neoliberal capitalism can only be exploded and moved beyond if, per cultural critic Steven Shaviro, we 'push it to its most extreme point, follow it into its furthest and strangest consequences.' In other words, a treatment by way of metastasis. The Tsai of *Walker* offers a protest that is, conversely, decelerationist. In his conviction that 'everything should be stopped,' Tsai is akin to the Benjamin who in the notes of his 1940 'On the Concept of

History' writes, 'Marx says that revolutions are the locomotive of world history. But perhaps it is quite otherwise. Perhaps revolutions are an attempt by the passengers on this train – namely, the human race – to activate the emergency brake.'

As revolutions go, Tsai shows more evident interest in the turnings of the dharma wheel than the coming of a proletarian paradise, but in his call to pull the brake he has something in common with his fellow flâneurs. The very existence of the flâneur, as White describes, relies on a dislocation from the cult of measurable productivity:

> By definition endowed with enormous leisure, someone who can take off a morning or afternoon for undirected ambling, since a specific goal or a close rationing of time is antithetical to the true spirit of the *flâneur*. An excess of the work ethic (or a driving desire to see everything and meet everyone of recognized value) inhibits the browsing, cruising ambition to 'wed the crowd'.

Delany, whose cruising adventures constitute a long litany of honeymoons with the crowd, delineates the difference between two kinds of social encounter: 'networking', which occurs within groups united by predetermined commonalities, and 'contact', which occurs across bounds of class, race, religion and so forth. What is increasingly in peril for Delany, as for Tsai, is the disappearance of the public spaces that create the potential for contact – even if, as in *Goodbye, Dragon Inn*, that contact is ultimately deferred, abortive.

Networking, dealing as it does in meetings of 'recognized value', is the priority in a city that values only what can be monetised – a phenomenon with implications that extend beyond urban planning into the very organisation of coincidence-and-risk-averse modern life, from entertainment (consumers are kept within algorithmically determined filter bubbles) to sexual relations (app-based selection minimising odd and accidental encounters). The category of happenstantial contact, in which Delany includes cruising, contributes to the intangible but invaluable qualities of life that the author dubs 'pleasantness'. Crucial to Tsai's conception of cinema, be it in a movie theatre, a gallery or a coffee shop screening room, is a belief in the possibility of such contact. His idea of a public space that produces opportunities for encounter and exchange – of dreams, of sex, of pears on a skewer – encourages hope, false though that hope may ultimately prove to be, that the loneliness of urban existence may be assuaged.

With this in mind, the Golden Age of Tsai's youth, a world in which you could 'go to the cinema twice a day, every day' and opt to 'watch the same film over and over again', may seem to have as much to do with the availability of leisure time to see films as with the films that were seen. It's no coincidence that the new cultural primacy of "content" designed for home viewing has coincided with the enforcement of an always-on-call work culture – how many people of modest means today have the time and money for such luxuriant moviegoing? The replacement of the neighbourhood cinema by the destination multiplex makes going to the movies an event, a time-absorbing commitment, while the social, communal experience loses ever more ground to the isolated binge-watch. The hype surrounding the "home theatre" experience, and the concomitant praise of new, serious-minded serial dramas, rather conveniently correlates to the expectations of the managerial class – a worker who is away at the movies can't be counted on to answer their emails. It has happened so subtly, and so quietly, that few noticed the incursion until it was too late. 'Our lifestyles have changed,' Tsai has said. 'But very few people think about the changes.'

Tsai, like Delany's cruiser, like most any artist, seeks his own points of contact – in this case with an audience – but the venues for these encounters grow increasingly scarce. Even *Stray Dogs*, Tsai's last feature film to have something like a traditional theatrical run, was given an unorthodox rollout in Taiwan. After winning the Grand Jury Prize in Venice, said Tsai, a theatrical release was expected, but,

> I didn't want to ... I wanted to show it just for my fans. So I organized 50 screenings on a single screen. Ten thousand people saw the film, then I stopped. After, I moved it to a special museum installation with three different rooms, so people could experience it in a different setting, in a different way. Then I stopped again, and decided

> that I wasn't going to do a DVD release or sell it to TV, that this was the only way the film should be seen. I wanted a concept where you saw the film through its author's eyes.

The somewhat tetchy relationship between non-commercial Taiwanese filmmakers and the exhibitors and audiences in their native country is not without precedent – Edward Yang, who'd spent many years in the US, was perennially bemoaning the difficulty of reviving a market for "art" cinema in Taiwan, and Hou, per *All Corners of the World*, was no competition for Schwarzenegger and Jackie Chan. For Tsai, the struggle today is to accustom an audience to accept the gallery space as a venue for cinema:

> I hope I can view Taiwan as a starting point to cultivate an audience, by showing films in the museum, making an exhibition, or even making films for the museum. You see, film needs an audience in the movie theater, and it's the same for the museum. However, I am also an Asian – I think people are not encouraged to visit museums in Asia. It's not a habit. Those who want to watch films will only go to the movie theater.

Tsai has also explored having his work seen without any set venue at all. The second *Walker* film was produced under the auspices of the Hong Kong International Film Festival Society, one of four short films banded together as *Beautiful 2012*, and hosted on the Chinese equivalent to YouTube, Youku, where it racked up scads of mixed comments. Free and easy access, as is often the case, brought with it the rowdiness one encounters when leaving Axël's castle and the rarefied air of the physical exhibition space: 'There have been more than four million clicks to see the video,' said Tsai, 'but an even greater number of people wrote in to complain about it. They said they found it unbearable, that Lee Kang-sheng was walking too slowly, that someone should push him, or hit him on the head to make him react.' (A curious side effect of open access: a level of vituperation rarely encountered from paying customers, the wrathful indignity of the freeloader!)

The cross-pollination of the film and gallery worlds has produced some exemplary works – works that might not have existed, or existed in very different form, without institutional backing.

My own optimism regarding the possibility of the gallery as a haven for "difficult" cinema, however, is not so great as Tsai's. Despite the myriad compromises built into the systems through which films are financed and exhibited, the traditional dependence on rapport with a popular audience has kept cinema free of the perfectly insidious financial arrangements that define the gallery world, which depends in no small part on catering to the whims of a handful of obscenely wealthy international collectors. And while I find much to respect in Tsai's *Walker* films, I can't dispense entirely with the feeling that they lack a force and feeling to be found in his fiction feature undertakings. I am not certain if this loss should be attributed to venue, or to format. I don't know that I would maintain, as Mangolte does, that the digital image is 'unable to establish and construct an experiential sense of time passing,' though I am convinced that the influence of conceptual art on cinema has not been an entirely salubrious one. Very often this is the stressing of "concept" in the singular, which can prove rather onerous over the course of a feature-length film, designed to carry the weight of a full narrative arc. (McQueen's features exemplify this.) All of which stands in contrast to Truffaut's maxim, written to screenwriter Jean Gruault in the margins of the script for *The Wild Child* (1970): 'I don't want one idea every four minutes, I want four ideas every one minute!'

In second-guessing Tsai, however, I am well aware that I am contending with a figure who has understood the coming changes in his medium better than most, and wonder to what degree I might be clinging to a reactionary conception of cinema rooted in a receding past. Tsai may be a decelerationist but he is by no means conservative – nor were his models. Prior to becoming filmmakers, Truffaut and his cohort were inspired by the ideas articulated in an influential 1948 essay by Alexandre Astruc, titled 'The Birth of a New Avant-Garde: The Camera-Pen'. A decade before *The 400 Blows* and more than a half-century before *Goodbye, Dragon Inn*, Astruc already foresaw cinema beyond the cinema:

> It must be understood that up to now the cinema has been nothing more than a show. This is due to the basic fact that all films are projected

> in an auditorium. But with the development of 16mm and television, the day is not far off when everyone will possess a projector, will go to the local bookstore and hire films written on any subject, of any form, from literary criticism and novels to mathematics, history, and general science. From that moment on, it will no longer be possible to speak of *the* cinema. There will be *several* cinemas just as today there are several literatures, for the cinema, like literature, is not so much a particular art as a language which can express any sphere of thought.

In the years following *Goodbye, Dragon Inn*, Tsai has dedicated himself to exploring the several cinemas that comprise twenty-first century moving image-based art, and in doing so has entirely reconsidered and reconfigured the nature of his work. For a self-confessed nostalgic, Tsai has proven remarkably receptive to new technologies, and with *The Deserted* even made a foray into the terrain of virtual reality. The 55-minute piece in question premiered at the Venice Film Festival in 2017, at a moment when film festivals were desperate to get into the VR business, and was produced by HTC, the Taiwan-based electronics company whose Vive VR headset was intended as a direct competitor to the Oculus Go, PlayStation VR and Samsung Gear VR. (While independent filmmakers struggle to scrape together a few shekels for "traditional" works, venture capital has been optimistically poured into VR by the millions, but thus far the predictions of a time when VR parlours would fill up abandoned multiplexes have proven only wishful thinking on the part of Silicon Valley investors.)

More typical of Tsai's current practice, though, are the *Walker* films, which Tsai declared were pivotal in his development as an artist. 'I discovered that with these films I'm more like a painter,' he has said of the series. 'I wanted to throw away people's concepts of what films are supposed to be, my concepts of what films are supposed to be. I realised that films can be truly precise, handmade craftsmanship. When I realised that, my anxiety just disappeared.'

For Tsai, then, the sadness of bidding goodbye to the classical theatrical experience that he'd grown up with is counterbalanced by the excitement of reimagining cinema, of finding it in new venues. In his resistance to existing exhibition paradigms, at least, Tsai is a dissident force – but his is a quiet rebellion, commanding in its calm. And his rebellion contains a surrender, one which in its terms might agree with Miguel de Cervantes, writing in the voice of the 'Muslim philosopher' and narrator of *Don Quixote*, Cide Hamete:

> To believe that the things of this life will endure forever, unchanged, is to believe the impossible; it seems instead that everything goes around, I mean around in a circle: spring pursues summer, summer pursues *estío*, *estío* pursues autumn, autumn pursues winter, and winter pursues spring, and in this way time turns around a continuous wheel; only human life races to its end more quickly than time, with no hope for renewal except in the next life, which has no boundaries that limit it.

11.

The invention without a future's lifespan now straddles three centuries, making the cinema a rather venerable hopeless case. Not a year has passed since its birth when it hasn't been pronounced dead, and in *Goodbye, Dragon Inn* we find one of its most eloquent and plangent eulogies. But for Tsai, we must remember, death is not the end. And if a man can die and be reincarnated as a fish, might not cinema die in the cinema and be reincarnated as a multi-channel installation, a URL, an AirDrop?

Jones, discussing cinema's marginalisation, writes that 'the cinema is no more in danger of dying now than it was twenty years ago when Susan Sontag diagnosed its terminal phase. Rather, it's the conditions of its existence, which we have long mistaken for the art form itself, that have changed.' Tsai's career subsequent to *Goodbye, Dragon Inn* shows an embrace of these changing conditions of existence – when *Stray Dogs* was shown in Taiwan galleries, the director described it thus: 'We made the projection screen out of crumpled paper used to cover the stage. Each shot was a separate projection, and audiences could go up and touch the screens. At times like these, don't you feel like cinema has been liberated?'

The projection, like Tsai's massive Chiang Kai-shek on Kinmen Island, gazing towards the Mainland, would be defined as a site-specific work – and site-specificity is a category from which the cinema, traditionally, has been barred admission. Following the line laid out by Benjamin in his essay 'The Work of Art in the Age of Mechanical Reproduction', the projected film, by virtue of the film print's reproducibility, is denied the element of 'aura' – a property belonging to those singular art objects possessed of a 'unique existence at the place where it happens to be', though jeopardised by the rise of mechanical reproduction: the photograph, the movie camera. The paintings seen hanging in the Louvre in *Faces* may have sustained something of their aura despite countless reproductions; a print of the film, by Benjamin's reckoning, never had it in the first place.

Something curious has happened, however, in the years following the DCP changeover; as the film print faced its first real threat of obsolescence, its own unique existence became evident in a way that had too long been overlooked. A DCP, variables of projection quality notwithstanding, will be the same DCP on its first or its thousandth projection. The 4K restoration of *Goodbye, Dragon Inn* introduced in Venice will look much the same anywhere around the world and, in lieu of circulating prints or a new restoration – and with restoration resources strained, these things have an air of finality about them – it will constitute the definitive version of the film, free of variables of attrition through projection and lab work, unchanging, its virtues and flaws unfaded forevermore. (The hazard, of course, is that once a digital restoration comes along it tends to be regarded as definitive, and shoddy ones – of which there are a great many – forestall future improvements.)

The practical advantages of distributing and exhibiting movies on DCP are self-evident. The argument for the film print is one to be made less on the behalf of pragmatic purposes than for intangibles, of certain qualities of the image lost in the digital changeover, even, yes, the disappearance of aura. The experience of seeing a print projected is one of the sources of what Delany describes as pleasantness, those barely perceptible properties that are especially vulnerable to the chopping block when art is submitted to the logic of profit margins and account books.

Perhaps it is natural for every generation to pity a little the generations who follow them, as Tsai seemed to when he told *The Guardian*, 'In my childhood, cinema was like going into a temple. Now, it's more like going into a shopping mall.' In some cases this pity takes the form of a convinced pessimism, as in the Cassandra-like opening to Schrader's *The Canyons*. The same 2007 omnibus that contains *It's a Dream* also features David Cronenberg's morbidly comic *At the Suicide of the Last Jew in the World in the Last Cinema in the World*, in which the director is found holed-up in a disused movie theatre lavatory, prodding his head with a firearm while two callous television news reporters narrate and gloat over his final moments.

By contrast, Tsai has been almost optimistic about his prospects: 'In Asia right now, my audiences are more people in their teens and 20s than people of my generation. Maybe it's because they are the internet generation, they see so much information every day. So when they experience my films they maybe feel something different. They have no baggage about "what is film?"' *Goodbye, Dragon Inn* might be Tsai's attempt to shed that baggage himself, to start looking for the future of the invention without a past. At a masterclass on the occasion of a 2019 mini-retrospective at the Tate Modern, he would ask of the 'mysterious invention' that is cinema: 'is the frame a limitation, or an encouragement to extend into the beyond?'

If change of one kind or another is ineluctable, Tsai has as his means of resistance the cinematic apparatus. The neighbourhood theatre has much company among Tsai's gallery of ghosts. 'It seems that many places I shot for my films have vanished,' he told the *Taipei Times*. And don't make plans to visit the mural inside the abandoned building that concludes *Stray Dogs*. Per Tsai, 'The ruins were still there when we finished shooting, but now ... the building was torn down. So, in a sense, you can say that Kao's mural is preserved in my film.'

Stray Dogs ends with two shots, both sustained considerably past the point of comfort. The first, a medium two-shot, shows a man and a woman (Lee and Lu Yi-ching) standing in a dilapidated room, splashed with blue moonlight, looking at... something. She stares ahead intently. As she does, a tear rolls down her face, getting halfway before it halts and dries. He is less focused, sipping steadily from an airline bottle of booze, finally moved to lurch into an awkward embrace with her. What are they looking at? We have some idea from the shot sequence that preceded this, from the drop ceiling tiles visible in the background, some of them sagging, some of them gone. We've seen this building, those tiles, this room before. The next image, a medium long shot of the couple taken from behind and from an elevated vantage, confirms this is the same place, that they are audience to the same image. On the far wall, which has approximately the dimensions of a widescreen frame, someone has drawn a seaside horizon. The graffito depicts the rim of the ocean, a rocky shore, the forest line, mountains and the sky above. Though the woman has seemed more engaged by the image, she is the first to leave the room. The man lingers just a while longer, alone.

Working in charcoal and using the walls of derelict buildings as his canvases, the artist Kao Jun-Honn reproduced a series of photographs of Liugui in southern Taiwan taken by John Thomson, a Scotsman, in 1871. Captured in Tsai's film, another serendipitous location scouting find, Kao's work feels both modern and prehistoric; the graffito is cinematic in its widescreen scope, while its presentation evokes Paleolithic cave painting. 'By placing the exhibition space in an abandoned area,' Kao writes, describing the project for the

2013 Asian Art Biennial, 'the images would garner the potential to become backdrops and would thus take on more empty film set or theater-like qualities.'

One more moment of watching the watchers in Tsai's cinema, *Stray Dogs*'s final shots are images of desolation and commiseration – desolation in the sagging, sodden surroundings, but commiseration in the sharing of an experience, of stopping and seeing something, really seeing it, together. Kao's mural suggests the shore of a strange land, the excitement of beginning a journey, as Hu might have felt seeking his independence away from Hong Kong, as Tsai might have felt arriving as a young qiaosheng from Kuching. A sense of intolerable loss hangs over this final scene, and yet that shore holds out the potential of a utopia – or, more likely, the terrifying, electrifying prospect of starting all over again.

If cinema is dying remains to be seen. As to if we are dying, and if all of us will die, is a question that should inspire less debate. Closely connected to Tsai's interest in using cinema to provide a durational document is a fascination with the camera's ability to mark the passage – and ravages – of time, something that is at the centre of his long project with Lee. Said Tsai:

> As we have continued to collaborate, Lee has aged and his body has changed a lot. Usually in the film industry, when an actor ages and changes, the director will get a different actor to perform. Rather than choose that path, I chose to accept these changes and to allow the audience to watch as someone gets old and sometimes gets sick. I am using the changes in the body of Lee to have a conversation with the world. He will always be my actor. Using Lee throughout my career has been a kind of constraint because I could easily have used other professional or 'star' actors. Placing this constraint upon myself was an active choice: a choice that was not driven by market forces but by what I wanted to achieve in my films.

Each of Tsai's films, then, represents a marker in the lifeline of Lee Kang-sheng, like the rings on the redwood that Kim Novak points to in *Vertigo* (1958): 'Here I was born, and there I died.'

Through Tsai's cinema we have watched Lee grow into middle age, from the slender youth of *Boys* to the man of *Days*, now wearing a slight paunch, his face lined, his accumulated aches and pains temporarily alleviated through acupuncture therapy, and a deep tissue massage by a younger man (Anong Houngheuangsy) which precedes a sexual encounter. So inextricable is the tie between Tsai's cinema and Lee's presence, so intent is Tsai's abiding interest in recording the effects of time and tide, even the incremental progress that is made in the *Walker* films attains new significance as we become aware that we're seeing a portion of a man's life passing before us. (A quote from Jean Cocteau may be apposite: 'Since the day of my birth, my death began its walk. It is walking towards me, without hurrying.')

Along with tracking Lee's gradual aging from film to film, Tsai has a penchant for juxtapositions that starkly illustrate the pitilessness of passing years. Here is a bustling Fu-Ho Grand; there is its husk. Here is Jean-Pierre Léaud at age fourteen in *The 400 Blows*; there he is at almost sixty in *What Time Is It There?* Here are Shih Chun and Miao

Tien as robust young xia heroes in King Hu's *Dragon Inn*; there they are as bent, forgotten men in *Goodbye, Dragon Inn*.

Tsai may be an acolyte of Hu, but in some crucial regards he is also his antonym. In one striking shot in *A Touch of Zen*, when Han Ying-jie's Commander Xu Xian-chun springs to attack, his impossible leap is rendered through a sly jump cut. To expedite the journey of a body in motion through the excising of a few frames would be, by contrast, wholly foreign to Tsai's mindset; he endeavours to show us the whole hobbling journey of a lamed usherette, the decelerated progress of a monk through a buzzing urban centre or, in *Days*, a static camera scene of food preparation that is almost *Jeanne Dielman*-like. Across his cinema, we have watched, too, Taipei torn down and rebuilt, and an art form, once in rude health, now clinging to life in its dotage.

Cinema was born in the rush and push of the turn of the newly electrified last century. Its continued existence – at least as a popular art, or an art at all – is threatened in a new century that is no less frantic in its own way. Changes occur with reckless speed, the assumption being that by the time anyone has noticed, the moment for protest will have passed. Bob Mould's bellow on Hüsker Dü's 'Divide and Conquer' gets at the essence of this conniving velocity: 'It's not about my politics / Something happened way too quick / A bunch of men who played it sick / They divide, conquer.'

Against this, Tsai's gentle protest is perhaps too quiet to be heard above the din of ceaseless activity, but worth registering all the same. Through cinema, his films tell us, time can be held in abeyance for a moment, or can be studied over and over again in its passing; in the cinema, they tell us, 1967 can for a couple of hours link hands with 2003. And if time can be regained through cinema, who is to say that cinema will fare so poorly in the hands of time?

Chapter 1

11 *CGI broke the special relationship* – J. Hoberman, *Film After Film: Or, What Became of 21st Century Cinema?* (London and New York: Verso, 2012), 4

11 *guiding myth* – André Bazin, 'The Myth of Total Cinema', trans. Hugh Gray, *What Is Cinema? Vol. 1* (Berkeley and Los Angeles: University of California Press, 1967), 21

12 *the full potential of the cinema* – Kenneth Tynan, *The Diaries of Kenneth Tynan*, ed. John Lahr (London: Bloomsbury, 2001), 100

17 *the conversation about cinema* – Kent Jones, 'The Marginalization of Cinema', *Film Comment* 52, no.6 (November-December 2016), 54–59. All subsequent Kent Jones quotes are from this source.

19 *a time of crisis* – Paul Schrader, untitled contribution to the anthology film *Venezia 70 – Future Reloaded* (2013)

22 *more akin to amusement park rides than cinema* – Martin Scorsese, 'The Dying Art of Filmmaking', *New York Times* (5 November 2019), 27

Chapter 3

37 *I first saw Dragon Inn* – Tsai Ming-liang, quoted in Gary G. Xu, *Sinascape: Contemporary Chinese Cinema* (Lanham: Rowman & Littlefield, 2007), 89

38 *the biggest cinephiles I knew* – Tsai Ming-liang, 'Chasing the Film Spirit', trans. Aliza Ma, *Metrograph* 1 (Spring 2016), 27

40 *a dozen cinemas in which I lingered* – Tsai, 27

40 *one was Capitol* – Tsai, quoted in Xu, *Sinascape*, 89

40 *the ceiling was very high up* – Tsai Ming-liang, quoted in Chang Jinn-Pei, 'Goodbye, Dragon Inn', Groupement National des Cinémas de Recherche (online) (July 2004); author's translation

41 *Kuching's cinemas were its secular temples* – Alan Lau, 'Electric Shadows', *Kuching In & Out* (online) (19 December 2017)

43 *on weekends* – George Kuchar, *Reflections from a Cinematic Cesspool* (Berkeley: Zanja Press, 1997), 6

44 *to reconstruct my childhood* – Jean Eustache, quoted in Luc Moullet, 'Better to burn out than to fade away: Blue collar dandy', *Film Comment* 36, no. 5 (September-October 2000), 41

50 *his family, with its very classic Taiwanese structure* – Tsai Ming-liang, quoted in Nick Pinkerton, 'A More Beautiful Life: An Interview with Tsai Ming-liang', trans. Alissa Ma, *Reverse Shot* (online) (17 April 2015)

51 *I do not want the audience* – Tsai Ming-liang, quoted in Emilie Yueh-yu Yeh and Darrell William Davis, *Taiwan Film Directors: A Treasure Island* (New York: Columbia University Press, 2005), 248

51 *very early on* – Tsai Ming-liang, quoted in Rachel Cheung, 'Filmmaker Tsai Ming-liang on sexuality and being touched by a goddess', *Post Magazine* (online) (20 October 2016)

CHAPTER 4

60 *after declining popularity* – Tsai Ming-liang, quoted in Armond White, 'Last Chinese picture show', *The Press Gang: Writings on Cinema from New York Press, 1991–2011*, ed. Jim Colvill (New York: Seven Stories Press, 2020), 380

67 *whenever I hear the word cinema* – Roland Barthes, 'Leaving the Movie Theater', *The Rustle of Language*, trans. Richard Howarth (New York: Farrar, Strauss and Giroux, 1986), 346

71 *metacinematic cruising* – Nicholas de Villiers, 'Leaving the cinema: metacinematic cruising in Tsai Ming-liang's *Goodbye, Dragon Inn*', *Jump Cut* 50 (online) (Spring 2008)

72 *the Chinese word wu* – Sam Ho, 'From Page to Screen: A Brief History of Wuxia Fiction', *Heroic Grace: The Chinese Martial Arts Film*, ed. David Chute and Lim Cheng-sim (Los Angeles: Foundation Press, 2003), 13

76 *to extract from fashion* – Charles Baudelaire, *The Painter of Modern Life and Other Essays*, trans. John Mayne (London: Phaidon, 1964), 12

76 *that aimless stroller* – Edmund White, *The Flâneur: A Stroll Through the Paradoxes of Paris* (London: Bloomsbury Publishing, 2001), 16

76 *to be gay and cruise* – White, 145

77 *like many young people* – Samuel R. Delany, *Times Square Red, Times Square Blue* (New York: NYU Press, 1999), xii

79 *our cities are changing all the time* – Tsai Ming-liang, quoted in Nigel Andrews, 'Tsai Ming-liang talks about "Stray Dogs"', *Financial Times* (online) (21 September 2013)

Chapter 5

81 *another way of going to the movies* – Barthes, 'Leaving the Movie Theater', 349

84 *when I began to make films* – Tsai, 'Chasing the Film Spirit', 27

85 *nestled rather insalubriously* – Lau, 'Electric Shadows'

87 *a brilliant carp spirit* – Tsai, 'Chasing the Film Spirit', 27

91 *of identity, of relations and of history* – Marc Augé, *Non-Places: Introduction to an Anthropology of Supermodernity*, trans. John Howe (London and New York: Verso Books, 1995), 52

Chapter 6

96 *Mandarin films from Hong Kong* – Edward Yang, quoted in Michael Berry, *Speaking in Images: Interviews with Contemporary Chinese Filmmmakers* (New York: Columbia University Press, 2005), 285

100 *an unprecedented cultural phenomenon* – Ramona Curry, 'Bridging the Pacific with *Love Eterne*', in *China Forever: The Shaw Brothers and Diasporic Cinema*, ed. Poshek Fu (Urbana: University of Illinois Press, 2008), 177

101 *color wuxia offensive* – 'Shaw Launches "Action Era"', *Southern Screen* 92 (October 1965), 30–43

106 *before King Hu left Los Angeles* – Sarah Pillsbury, quoted in Kar Law, 'Remembering King Hu', *Transcending the Times: King Hu and Eileen Chang*, trans. Stephen Teo (Hong Kong: Hong Kong International Film Festival, 1998), 112

107 *I found an old cinema* – Tsai, 'Chasing the Film Spirit', 27

110 *we had just finished filming* – Lee Kang-sheng, quoted in Volker Hummel, 'The Missing: An Interview with Lee Kang-sheng', Senses of Cinema 32 (online) (July 2004)

111 *television doomed us to the Family* – Barthes, 'Leaving the Movie Theater', 346

112 *cinema must remain the occasion of a meeting* – Marc Augé and Tom Conley, *Casablanca: Movies and Memory* (Minneapolis: University of Minnesota Press, 2009), 49

113 *my first two hundred films* – François Truffaut, *The Films in My Life* (New York: Simon & Schuster, 1975), 3

Chapter 7

117 *he has created his own world* – Tsai Ming-liang, quoted in Nanouk Leopold, 'Confined Space. Interview with Tsai Ming-liang', *Senses of Cinema* 20 (online) (May 2002)

118 *something very unique about film* – Tsai Ming-liang, quoted in Erik Morse, 'Time & Again', trans. Vincent Cheng, *Frieze* 137 (online) (March 2011)

119 *trains passing in the night* – This oft-quoted line is spoken by François Truffaut, playing the character of the film director in *Day for Night*: 'Films are more harmonious than life. There are no traffic jams in films, no dead waits. Films move forward like trains, like trains in the night.'

124 *I have worked with you for twenty years* – Tsai Ming-liang, quoted in programme notes for 'I Sing While Walking: Tsai Ming-liang Stories and Songs', Tai Kwun Centre for Heritage and Arts (online) (November 2018)

124 *before he started to make feature films* – Lee Kang-sheng, quoted in Hummel, 'The Missing'

127 *I was the double for Linda Lin-dai* – Han Yingjie, quoted in 'Three Interviews', *The Fifth Hong Kong International Film Festival: A Study of the Hong Kong Swordplay Film 1945–1980*, ed. Shing-hon Lau (Hong Kong: Hong Kong International Film Festival, 1981), 212

128 *Jackie Chan is Fred Astaire* – Donald E. Westlake, quoted in Richard Corliss, 'Go west, Hong Kong', *Time* 147, no. 9 (26 February 1996), 67

128 *rhythmic theater* – David Bordwell, *Planet Hong Kong: Popular Cinema and the Art of Entertainment* (Cambridge and London: Harvard University Press, 2000), 224

129 *not only tired but jubilant* – Bordwell, 244–245

129 *lyrical absurdity* – Graham Greene, *The Pleasure Dome: The Collected Film Criticism 1935–40*, ed. John Russell Taylor (Oxford: Oxford University Press, 1980), 55–56

131 *that era of breathlessly accelerated tempo* – Bordwell, *Planet Hong Kong*, 162

132 *a literary as much as an action director* – Tsai Ming-liang, quoted in Matthew Thrift, 'Tsai Ming-liang: 90 minutes with the slow cinema master', *Sight & Sound* (online) (8 April 2019)

Chapter 8

138 *a very famous song* – Tsai Ming-liang, quoted in Chang, 'Goodbye, Dragon Inn'

141 *cheap songs* – Dennis Potter, quoted in Melvyn Bragg, 'Great interviews of the 20th century: We tend to forget that life can only be defined in the present tense', *The Guardian* (online) (12 September 2007)

142 *weapons that I use to confront the environment* – Tsai Ming-liang, quoted in David Walsh, 'An interview with Tsai Ming-liang, director of *The Hole*', World Socialist Web Site (online) (7 October 1998)

143 *the bygone era of pop culture* – Andrew Chan, 'Ecstatic Nostalgia: New Theater Work by Tsai Ming-liang', MUBI Notebook (online) (5 December 2011)

146 *there's a popular saying* – Hua Hsu, 'The Melancholy Pop Idol Who Haunts China', *The New Yorker* (online) (3 August 2015)

149 *consummate scavengers* – Simon Reynolds, *Retromania: Pop Culture's Addiction to Its Own Past* (New York: Faber & Faber, 2011), 328

149 *unlike digital formats* – Reynolds, 388

150 *prints that seem overgrown with jungle moss* – Manny Farber, 'Underground Films', *Farber on Film: The Complete Film Writings of Manny Farber*, ed. Robert Polito (New York: The Library of America, 2016), 489

151 *ache of longing* – Reynolds, *Retromania*, 396

152 *an uncritical confusion* – Delany, *Times Square Red*, 16

154 *creating an experiential sense of time* – Babette Mangolte, 'Afterward: A Matter of Time', *Camera Obscura, Camera Lucida: Essays in Honor of Annette Michelson*, ed. Richard Allen and Malcolm Turvey (Amsterdam: Amsterdam University Press, 2003), 263

154 *television in public* – Quentin Tarantino, quoted in Stephen Galloway and Matthew Belloni, 'Director Roundtable 6: Auteurs on Tantrums, Crazy Actors and Quitting While They're Ahead', *Hollywood Reporter* (online) (28 November 2012)

Chapter 9

159 *the background music of my youth* – Tsai Ming-liang, quoted in Chang, 'Goodbye, Dragon Inn'

160 *from my point of view* – Tsai, quoted in Pinkerton, 'A More Beautiful Life'

164 *if box-office numbers* – Tsai, quoted in Pinkerton

169 *to speak today of a famous novelist* – Gore Vidal, *Point to Point Navigation: A Memoir* (New York: Doubleday, 2006), 2

172 *I can't just be a lone flower* – Tsai Ming-liang, quoted in Huei-Yin Chen, 'Interview: Tsai Ming-liang', *Film Comment* (online) (6 April 2015)

173 *at that time* – Tsai, quoted in Pinkerton, 'A More Beautiful Life'

174 *many people from the art world* – Tsai, quoted in Chen, 'Interview'

175 *castration* – Tsai Ming-liang, quoted in Caroline Gluck, 'Art: Swords into art on Taiwan', *New York Times* (online) (15 September 2004)

175 *I went back to a cinema in Malaysia* – Tsai Ming-liang, quoted in Noah Buchan, 'Film's death and resurrection', *Taipei Times* (25 March 2010), 13

177 *a film about a rundown cinema* – Tsai, quoted in Buchan

178 *a vantage on not only the screen* – Erik Bordeleau, 'Soulful Sedentarity: Tsai Ming-liang at Home at the Museum', *Studies in European Cinema* 10, no. 2–3 (2003), 181

178 *these chairs are the remains of the cinema* – Tsai, quoted in Buchan, 'Film's death and resurrection'

179 *someone asked him* – Tsai, quoted in Pinkerton, 'A More Beautiful Life'

180 *a space where the cinema can go to be reborn* – Beth Tsai, 'The many faces of Tsai Ming-liang: Cinephilia, the French connection, and cinema in the gallery', *International Journal of Asia Pacific Studies* 13, no. 2 (2017), 146

180 *this movie announced the death of film* – Tsai, quoted in Buchan, 'Film's death and resurrection'

Chapter 10

185 *precipitating an analogous change* – Andrew V. Uroskie, *Between the Black Box and the White Cube: Expanded Cinema and Postwar Art* (Chicago: University of Chicago Press, 2014), 12

190 *a conscious act of rebellion* – Tsai Ming-liang, quoted in Maria Giovanna Vagenas, 'Filmmaker Tsai Ming-liang says his work should be appreciated slowly', *South China Morning Post* (online) (27 August 2013)

190 *life is business, life is competition* – Tsai Ming-liang, quoted in Erik Bordeleau, 'On the uses and misuses of cinema', Senses of Cinema 58 (online) (March 2011)

191 *push it to its most extreme point* – Steven Shaviro, *No Speed Limit: Three Essays on Accelerationism* (Minneapolis: University of Minnesota Press, 2015), 1

192 *revolutions are the locomotive of world history* – Walter Benjamin, *Selected Writings, 4: 1938–1940*, trans. Edmund Jephcott, ed. Howard Eiland and Michael W. Jennings (Cambridge: Belknap Press of Harvard University Press, 2003), 402

192 *endowed with enormous leisure* – White, *The Flâneur*, 39–40

195 *our lifestyles have changed* – Tsai, quoted in Buchan, 'Film's death and resurrection'

195 *I didn't want to* – Tsai, quoted in Thrift, 'Tsai Ming-liang'

196 *I hope I can view Taiwan* – Tsai, quoted in Chen, 'Interview'

197 *more than four million clicks* – Tsai, quoted in Vagenas, 'Filmmaker Tsai Ming-liang'

198 *an experiential sense of time passing* – Mangolte, 'Afterward', 263

199 *I don't want one idea every four minutes* – François Truffaut paraphrased by Arnaud Desplechin, quoted in Jared Rapfogel, 'One Idea Every Fifteen Seconds: An Interview with Arnaud Desplechin', *Cineaste* 30, no. 2 (Spring 2005), 34

199 *cinema has been nothing more than a show* – Alexandre Astruc, 'The Birth of a New Avant-Garde: The Camera-Pen', *The French New Wave: Critical Landmarks*, trans. Peter Graham, ed. Graham and Ginette Vincendeau (London: British Film Institute, 2009), 32

201 *I'm more like a painter* – Tsai, quoted in Thrift, 'Tsai Ming-liang'

202 *the things of this life will endure* – Miguel de Cervantes, *Don Quixote*, trans. Edith Grossman (London: Vintage, 2005), 804

CHAPTER 11

206 *we made the projection screen* – Tsai, quoted in Pinkerton, 'A More Beautiful Life'

206 *unique existence* – Walter Benjamin, 'The Work of Art in the Age of Mechanical Reproduction', *Illuminations*, trans. Harry Zohn, ed. Hannah Arendt (New York: Schocken Books, 1968), 220

208 *in my childhood* – Tsai Ming-liang, quoted in Steve Rose, 'Tsai Ming-liang: master of long takes and watermelon sex', *The Guardian* (online) (5 April 2019)

209 *in Asia right now* – Tsai, quoted in Rose

209 *mysterious invention*– Tsai Ming-liang, quoted in Elena Gorfinkel, '"To extend into the beyond": on Tsai Ming-liang's late digital style', *Sight & Sound* (online) (22 April 2019)

210 *many places I shot for my films have vanished* – Tsai Ming-liang, quoted in Yu Sen-lun, 'Tsai Ming-liang continues his search for vanishing Taipei', *Taipei Times* (online) (25 April 2003)

210 *the ruins were still there* – Tsai, quoted in Chen, 'Interview'

211 *placing the exhibition space in an abandoned area* – Kao Jun-Honn, quoted in programme notes for 'On-Site: Field Note for the Ruins', Asian Art Biennial (online) (16 November 2013)

213 *as we have continued to collaborate* – Lee Kang-sheng, quoted in Declan McGrath, 'Painterly Poetics: An Interview with Tsai Ming-liang and Lee Kang-sheng', *Cineaste* 44, no. 4 (Autumn 2019; web exclusive)

214 *since the day of my birth* – Jean Cocteau, 'La Fin du Potomak', *Œuvres complètes de Jean Cocteau; vol. 2*, (Geneva: Marguerat, 1947), 234; author's translation

About the author:
Nick Pinkerton is a Cincinnati-born, Brooklyn-based writer focused on moving image-based art. His writing has appeared in *Film Comment*, *Sight & Sound*, *Artforum*, *Frieze*, *Reverse Shot*, *The Guardian*, *4Columns*, *The Baffler*, *Rhizome*, *Harper's* and the *Village Voice*, among other venues, and he operates the Substack newsletter Employee Picks. Previous publications include the monograph *Mondo Cinema and Beyond, 196Øs–198Øs* (True/False).